THE LIVES OF LEAVES

THE LIVES
OF LEAVES

WHAT LEAVES MEAN – AND
WHAT THEY MEAN TO US

Dan Crowley and Douglas Justice

First published in Great Britain in 2021 by Two Roads
An Imprint of John Murray Press
An Hachette UK company

1

Hardback ISBN 978-1-529-37531-2
eBook ISBN 978-1-529-37533-6

Typeset in Kings Caslon by Palimpsest Book Production Ltd, Falkirk, Stirlingshire

Printed and bound in Great Britain by Clays Ltd, Elcograf S.p.A.

John Murray policy is to use papers that are natural, renewable
and recyclable products and made from wood grown in sustainable forests.
The logging and manufacturing processes are expected to conform to
the environmental regulations of the country of origin.

Two Roads
Carmelite House
50 Victoria Embankment
London EC4Y 0DZ

www.tworoadsbooks.com

CONTENTS

Contents

INTRODUCTION

The first thing we notice about trees – aside from their extraordinary variety, size, flowers or fruit – are their leaves. Large or small, they are usually a tree's most obvious feature. We are attracted to their greenness and in spring freshly emerging leaves signal abundance and the promise of increasing warmth in the days ahead. In autumn, the leaves of most temperate deciduous trees change colour with the cooler, shortening days, gradually falling and scattering.

Leaf size, shape and colour are the main features we use to get to know trees, but there are less obvious clues – their chemistry, toothing, vein architecture and vestiture, for example – that point to myriad connections between the various kinds of trees. Tree identification sometimes requires nothing more than a cursory glance (that's a willow and here's an oak), but often a much closer look is required.

Leaves reveal more than just an indication of their species. Shape and size might tell us what climate a tree is suited to, and their armature might give us a clue as to what might be eating them. Aroma could suggest a biochemical connection to another species entirely or, perhaps, remind you of the perfume of someone you used to know.

Trees are photoautotrophs: their leaves make food photosynthetically, using sunlight, water, carbon dioxide and minerals from the soil. The oxygen that life requires is a by-product of that process. That's lucky for us, and for this alone, leaves and the trees upon which they are borne deserve our respect. But of course, leaves are more than that. To animals and people, they are sources of food, medicine and shelter. Long the subjects of art, leaf patterns are commonly portrayed in ancient cultures; they continue as much today. In some places, leaves are even used to make musical instruments.

It is a sad fact that at least one in four tree species is now threatened with extinction in the wild. As much as we need them, they need our help. Unlike us, plants cannot get up and move to avoid predators. Instead, they have evolved countless ingenious methods to avoid being eaten. Unfortunately, though, there are plenty of threats that no amount of evolution can counter. Nearly everywhere trees are imperilled by unsustainable harvesting practices, habitat destruction and development. But if we can get to know our trees a little better, understand more about their amazing life histories and recognise the complex processes that allow them to survive and perform in their crucial roles in supporting ecosystems, perhaps we can make more of the positive changes needed to flick the switch.

There are many stories to tell: stories about the trees we might take for granted because they are so familiar, about those that are notorious because they are altogether too common and growing where they don't belong, as well as stories of some of the rarest and most singular of trees. This is why we chose to write this book. Trees, and their leaves, inspire us, and we hope that this book in turn inspires and encourages its readers. We've included stories of trees from all over the world. Several of our chosen species can be seen growing in the world's botanic gardens, which are ideal places to study leaves, or even just admire them. But there are many more trees and leaves to discover. This book does not attempt to explain everything there is to know about leaves, but we hope the reader might be tempted to delve a little deeper.

Out of thousands of choices we selected 50 trees with leaves that we personally considered most compelling. In this volume we focus on trees that have leaves with interesting chemistry and impressive (and sometimes improbable) defensive armature and other extraordinary features. We wanted to highlight the capacity of leaves to change shape and to act as homes and larders for insects, as well as serve as food for humans and other animals. We feature leaves that provide building materials and other objects of value. Some of our tree choices produce leaves that bestow healing medicines. A few species define the landscapes that they inhabit—a subset of those represent regrettable human-induced invasiveness and over-abundance. A good number of the trees herein are cultivated, and some are valued for their timber, while others – wild species – may be lost to us before the perceived value of leaving them standing catches up to our ability to save them. While there is plenty of overlap in features among the various examples – numerous trees have interesting chemistry, are enormously useful and are also effective in protecting them-selves – we have tried to organise the chapters to include trees that conform at least in part to the themes elucidated here.

WHAT REMARKABLE CHEMISTRY!

The diversity of the phenomena of nature is so
great, and the treasures hidden in the heavens so rich,
precisely in order that the human mind shall never be
lacking in fresh nourishment.

JOHANNES KEPLER

*Chemistry is the foundation of life, and of leaves. Before the advent
of molecular genetic (DNA) analysis, one of the most important
tools for distinguishing between species and especially larger plant
groups was the isolation and characterisation of phytochemicals,
plant chemicals found in the leaves. The two most apparent phyto-
chemical groups are pigments, including the ubiquitous
anthocyanins, and aromatic compounds, of which there is a huge
variety; think leaf scents, floral fragrances and conifer aromas.
In the tulip tree and sugar maple we discover that anthocyanins
have important but different seasonal roles, while anthocyanins
also determine whether a tree will be a green or copper beech.
Aromatic compounds are responsible for the candyfloss aroma of
katsura leaves, the smell of freshly mown grass around black
walnut leaves and the deadly toxins coursing through the leaves
and stems of the Mexican chamal. The versatility of neem, which
is almost too fantastic to believe (it is both an effective pesticide
and safe in toothpaste), comes down to the chemistry in its leaves
and wood. Clearly there is more to these plants than chemistry
alone, but just knowing that maple syrup is a product of photosynthesis should tell you that leaf chemistry is indeed remarkable.*

5

KATSURA

Cercidiphyllum japonicum

Native only to Japan and eastern China, though enormously popular landscape trees wherever they can be grown, katsuras were once much more widespread. *Cercidiphyllum* fossils are common in deposits laid down in North America, Greenland, western Europe and Siberia, which indicates that katsuras were present millions of years ago, well before humans were around to appreciate them.

A fast-growing deciduous tree – it is the tallest flowering tree in Asia – katsura has a broad, rounded crown and is readily recognised by its strongly ascending, often multiple stems, furrowed and twisted bark and tiered, well-spaced, sweeping branches. Katsuras are texturally unlike most other trees, growing tall with prominent bunches of radiating branches at the ends of main scaffold branches. As well, knobby 'short shoots' naturally develop along the branches, each bearing a single leaf in the growing season. Extension growth on these shoots is limited to a few millimetres annually. Much like in ginkgo (see page 245), the prominence of short shoots increases with age, giving the un-shaded interior branches of mature katsuras a leafy, well-clothed look in summer and a somewhat bumpy, but not unattractive appearance in winter.

The new leaves of most katsuras emerge copper or bronzy green, or even purple. Easily recognised because the leaves are rounded or heart shaped, they are not unlike those of the Judas tree or redbud (*Cercis*) – though much smaller – and it is from this similarity that we get the name *Cercidiphyllum*: *kerkis* = redbud + *phyllon* = leaf. The katsura's leaves have impressed veins and finely scalloped, recurved margins and they are borne in opposite to closely opposite pairs along the long, slender shoots. Leaves produced from short shoots are usually larger and more rounded. On close inspection, the leaves are exceptionally waxy, often bluish below, and they have a dry, potato-skin feel above, which causes rain to be shed in rivers of beads, the water never appearing to actually touch the leaf surface. The dull waxiness also seems to enhance the absorption and transmission of light through the canopy, rather than reflecting it away. Standing under the tree in bright sunshine, each leaf looks as though it's lit from within.

Variation in katsuras is mostly limited to lighter or darker emerging foliage in spring, as well as in overall crown shape. The darkest leaves are mostly produced by more variable Chinese plants (sometimes listed as *C. japonicum* var. *sinense*). A few horticultural selections have been made from Chinese seedlings, and 'Rotfuchs' (German for 'red fox') has small leaves that are nearly purple-black when new, that fade to maroon as they mature. Trees of Japanese provenance are typically more predictably uniform in leaf shape and colour. Perhaps the most famous of all katsuras, though, is an ancient Japanese clone known from before 1635, called 'Morioka Weeping'. An elegant, weeping tree with strongly upright primary shoots and gracefully cascading side branches, 'Morioka Weeping' can become very tall and wide-spreading, not unlike a weeping beech (*Fagus sylvatica* Pendula Group) in habit. Modern stocks are all derived from an individual plant collected at the Ryugenzi Temple near the city of Morioka in northern Japan. Although plants with pendulous stems and coloured leaves are common in gardens – and there are several other weeping selections, as well as yellow-leaved katsura cultivars – such mutations are vanishingly rare in the wild.

Few pests ever seem to bother the katsura, although you may occasionally spot the perfectly cut circles of leafcutter bees (*Megachile* species), though these do little damage, and echo the rounded arcs of the leaf edges. The nests of opportunistic tent caterpillars (*Malacasoma* species) sometimes appear in the crowns of katsuras, but infestations of these otherwise ubiquitous and gastronomically flexible pests are rare, and, together with the leafcutters, they are usually the limit of insect visitation. Diseases, too, are uncommon in katsura. Though there appears to be little research on the subject, the chemistry of these trees is obviously exceptional in keeping foliage feeders and pathogenic microbes away. If you do spot dead or dying katsura in the landscape, then, these are invariably drought-stressed trees, as their requirement for water is as remarkable as their usual good health.

Cercidiphyllum species are dioecious (i.e. there are separate male and female trees) and the tiny flowers are wind-pollinated.

In spring, leaf emergence is preceded by the opening of hundreds of tiny, scarlet flowers on the short shoots that line the mature branches. The finest of spring days start by seeing the flowers catching the morning sun, like so many miniature rubies. On female trees, the fertilised flowers turn into clusters of up-standing seed capsules, like tiny bunches of bananas, filled with tinier winged seeds. In August, the drying capsules split open and thousands of tiny, whirling seeds float to the ground over a period of only a few days.

Although shaded plants are typically less flamboyant, the leaves of open-grown plants glow in modest, fiery tones of yellow, coral pink, red and black-purple in autumn, often turning one branch at a time. If that wasn't enough to recommend it, the senescing leaves of katsuras smell of burnt sugar – strawberries, ripe apples or candyfloss to some – a deliciously pervasive fragrance around any specimen at that time, as well as when leaves are shed during summer dry spells. If the technical explanation doesn't ruin the mystery and allure, the sugary smell is provided by the production of maltose (an aromatic sugar), when stored starches are broken down in the leaves. In the garden, people naturally slow down or even come to a stop as the aroma hits them, but most have no idea that dying leaves could be the source of such a wonderful smell.

CHAMAL

Dioon edule

Chamal, or dameu, is a small tree and a cycad, an ancient and extraordinary lineage of cone-bearing gymnosperms related to conifers and ginkgo (*Ginkgo biloba*). Fossil evidence shows that cycads were established more than 300 million years ago – well before the age of the dinosaurs. Cycads were at their most diverse during the Jurassic period (approximately 201.3 to 145 million years ago), when gymnosperms were the dominant form of vegetation globally, though they now comprise only 2 families and 350 or so species distributed across tropical and subtropical parts of the world.

Instead of having flowers with ovules (unfertilised seeds) enclosed in an ovary as occurs in angiosperms (flowering plants), gymnosperms have ovules that develop 'naked', on what are technically modified leaves or scales that are often fused into cones. 'Gymnosperm' comes from Greek and translates as 'naked seed'.

To the uninitiated, and without the benefit of cones – these can attain near barrel-like dimensions and weigh more than 25 kilograms – cycads could be confused with palms, their pinnate leaves held in tight rosettes recalling the foliar arrangement of some palm trees. Indeed, several cycads are referred to as 'palms' in local vernacular. In many areas they are also used similarly, for example for thatching, as the raffia palms are used (see palmier raffia, page 93). As their flower and fruiting structures suggest, however, the two groups are not closely related and their foliar similarities are a result of convergence, both having arrived, evolutionarily speaking, at similar designs from different starting places. As in the palms, there are a few cycads that have subterranean stems; others develop short trunks and remain diminutive. Around a third of all cycads are bona fide trees.

A close comparison of palm and cycad foliar features also reveals some differences. While the leaves of both palms and cycads are spirally arranged, palm leaf scars nearly completely encircle the stem or trunk, while those of cycads are diamond or lens shaped and the leaf bases more tightly packed. Cycad leaves also unfurl, much like the 'fiddleheads' of ferns, rather than expanding from flattened, folded, origami-like embryonic versions of themselves, as palms do. Although 'dicotyledonous' primarily refers to a category of flowering plants, cycads are also technically dicotyledonous, producing a pair of seed leaves upon germination. Palms, on the other hand, are proper flowering plants, and monocotyledonous, producing a single seed leaf.

Around 20 per cent of cycad species, including chamal, are native to Mexico, and like most of the world's cycads, they are threatened with extinction. As well as loss of habitat and the pressures of agriculture and climate change, they are also a target for poachers. Having survived for some 300 million years, cycads' biggest threat today is the illicit nursery trade. Collectors knowingly purchase these plants with an evident disregard not only for the law, but also the fragile habitats in which cycads naturally occur. A few species, now extinct in the wild, are currently only represented by cultivated specimens. The most well-known of these orphans is the South African Wood's cycad (*Encephalartos woodii*), which is represented in gardens by clones, as the species has only ever been known from a single male specimen. As all cycads are dioecious – with separate male and female plants – Wood's cycad is incapable of reproducing sexually, so is functionally, and thus effectively, extinct.

In several cultures, cycad seeds have been, and in many cases continue to be, important food sources, particularly during times of hardship and famine. For the Xi'iuy people of Mexico, chamal has long been part of their diet, used as an alternative to maize, with a dough made from the ground seeds for tamale, gordita and tortilla wraps. The specific epithet, *edule*, translates as 'edible', in reference to its use for food. Caution is however required, as many parts of cycads are poisonous, and plant parts are usually carefully processed to remove the toxins. The tissues surrounding the starchy chamal seed are highly toxic, for example. Complete removal of this covering, known as a sarcotesta, renders them edible. But detoxification processes are not always thoroughly executed. In the Ryukyu Islands of southern Japan, the seeds of the Japanese sago palm (*Cycas revoluta* – a cycad, and not a palm) are fermented and used to make a potent alcoholic beverage that remains slightly poisonous, although some particularly strong batches have actually proven fatal to those who have consumed it. It is aptly known as *doku* (poison) sake. And that's not to mention the hazards of acquiring the seeds in the first place. The venomous habu viper (*Protobothrops flavoviridis*), which is endemic to the Ryukyus, makes a nest amid the leaves of the Japanese sago palm and lays its eggs on the seeds. For those collecting seeds, choosing an occupied plant could result in an even more untimely death.

The Mexican chamal lacks a resident snake but, like many cycads, is not short on character. Its stout trunk is topped with a tight crown of up to 30 or so long, light green, pinnate leaves, each with up to an impressive 160 leaflets. Usually spineless along their margins, the leaflets are each tipped with a sharp point. Seed-cones are more modestly proportioned than in some cycads, though still more than a foot long. The largest cycad cone, at 80 centimetres long, belongs to another Mexican *Dioon* species, *D. spinulosum*.

Individual specimens of chamal have been estimated to be as much as 2,000 years old. With an average growth rate of 1.7 millimetres a year, and typically growing under tough, arid conditions, a plant might only become 2–3 metres tall in the wild but, by their second millennium, most certainly arborescent.

In its habitat, chamal has been much collected, but is also jeopardised by habitat loss, and is on the watch list of cycad conservators focused on minimising threats to its wild populations. Cattle farming threatens the species, as its toxic seeds and young leaves are attractive to livestock, with the simplest solution often deemed to be removal of the plants from grazing land. Consumption of the tender leaves firstly causes sickness in the cows, then paralysis of their hind legs, followed by death. The plant's toxicity is thus a highly effective defence against herbivory, though as agriculture has increased, it is the plants that are losing out. Where chamal is still harvested for food among Xi'iuy and mestizo communities, however, livestock and chamal manage to coexist, with cows housed away from plants until leaves are mature and less palatable.

While toxicity represents one aspect of its survival strategy, chamal employs a further adaptation to contend with aridity – a metabolic pathway common to many desert plants, but apparently unique among cycads. When short of water, chamal uses a modified photosynthetic pathway known as crassulacean acid metabolism (CAM). Instead of having stomata open during the day, plants open them only at night and thus largely prevent water loss through the day. Leaves are able to absorb and concentrate carbon dioxide during the night before using it the next day for photosynthesis. Named after the succulent-leaved crassulas (*Crassula* species) in which the mechanism was first identified, CAM photosynthesis is almost exclusively found in angiosperms and is characteristic of cacti and many other desert plants. The only other gymnosperm known to employ CAM is *Welwitschia mirabilis*, a unique, ground-hugging, long-lived and long-leaved species from the Namib Desert in southern Africa.

Aside from the botanical notoriety of this adaptive trait, the leaves of chamal, and those of other *Dioon* species, have special significance to people in Mexico and elsewhere in Central America. They are frequently used for decorative purposes in religious celebrations and are particularly associated with *Día de los Muertos* – Day of the Dead – a colour-filled show of love and respect for deceased family members that takes place on 1 and 2 November (All Saints' Day and All Souls' Day in the Catholic calendar). The modern festivities are an amalgamation of pre-Hispanic religious traditions and Christian feasts. Central to household or community celebrations is an *ofrenda*, an altar, which is ornately decorated to welcome the spirits of those passed back into the home. Where available, among showy flowers the leaves of chamal or other *Dioon* species are used as part of the display.

In parts of Honduras, the leaves of tiusinte (*Dioon mejiae*) are employed similarly, and also used to make wreaths to mark the graves of children. Painted or glittery wreaths may be taken to the cemetery as part of Day of the Dead festivities, though in some places paper or plastic alternatives are now used. Churches are also decked with tiusinte leaves to signify Holy Week (between Palm Sunday and Easter), and are used in nativity scenes as well as to mark Independence Day on 15 September.

These cycad leaf traditions are believed to pre-date the arrival of Christianity in Mesoamerica, and it is thought that the durable and manipulable nature of *Dioon* leaves is a key reason for their use, while they also retain their colour long after they have been cut, so are effective as part of multi-day festive displays. So important are the plants for traditional celebrations and observances that they are grown by communities in order to always have leaves available. A reverence among those who know the species might just be their best hope of survival.

TULIP TREE

Liriodendron tulipifera

Tulip tree is among the most recognisable of temperate deciduous hardwood tree species. Its specimens represent the largest old-growth trees remaining in the deciduous forests of eastern North America. It is the second largest hardwood in the whole of North America – only black cottonwood (*Populus trichocarpa*) beats it. A statuesque tulip tree trunk, with its leaves almost in the clouds, is a sight to behold. Besides its great size, the tulip tree stands out for the shape of its leaves, which have long, slender petioles, are deep green above and have a paler undersurface. They are broad, with a pair of large basal lobes and a smaller set at the apex, giving them a distinctive shape not seen in any other temperate tree genus.

The overwintering buds of the tulip tree are distinctive too, and specimens are readily identifiable by their buds alone. Appearing somewhat duck-billed, they comprise a pair of partially fused, near oblong-shaped stipules, flattened toward the tip. These fall away in late spring, exposing a tiny developing leaf inside. Unexpanded leaves are folded lengthwise and bent over. This folding and packing is known as conduplicate vernation – conduplicate is the botanical term for longitudinal folding, and vernation for how leaves are arranged in bud. Looking closely, a second, much smaller stipular bud is visible below the leaf. And inside this bud is another, tinier leaf with another even smaller stipular bud. This pattern continues for as many leaves as will be unfurled. The stipules fall away as the shoot expands, leaving a shallow crease that encircles the stem below each petiole, but by winter, these lines are barely visible below the D-shaped petiole scars.

Liriodendron is the only genus other than *Magnolia* in the magnolia family, Magnoliaceae. Along with the American species, there is another, the Chinese tulip tree (*Liriodendron chinense*), which occurs across temperate and subtropical parts of central and southern China, as well as neighbouring northern Vietnam. Aside from differing pigmentation on the inside of their tulip-like flowers (hence the common name), not a great deal separates them, apart from around 8,000 miles. Their leaves are similar, though with some subtle differences; the leaves can be slightly larger in the Chinese tulip tree, and are also, in young specimens at least, more 'narrow-waisted' than in the American version. However, these characteristics are not always consistent and there is considerable overlap in leaf shape and size between the two species. Fossil evidence indicates that they diverged approximately sixty-five million years ago, about the time North America and Eurasia broke apart.

The two tulip trees are at their most distinguishable in spring, when the leaves of the Chinese tulip tree exhibit shades of deep purple before turning green. This strong coloration is due to a concentration of anthocyanins in the leaf, with their presence most apparent before appreciable volumes of chlorophyll are produced.

Anthocyanins are a group of pigments found throughout the plant kingdom, showing up as the oranges, reds, purples and blues in leaves, flowers, fruits and stems (the word itself derives from the Greek *anthos*, for flower, and *kyanos*, blue). These pigments play numerous roles, including, famously, facilitating many aspects of reproduction. Colourful flowers and fruits attract pollinators and seed dispersers, for example. But anthocyanins also provide chemical protection from stressors both living and non-living, though their actual role in plant–environment interactions, particularly in established leaves, roots and stems, remains contentious. Mixtures of anthocyanins have distinctly different benefits depending on the plant species and the stage of growth.

On the other hand, the role of anthocyanins in fresh spring foliage is well understood, as they play a key role in defence. The ways in which they defend, however, are diverse. Firstly, they help to protect the chloroplasts, the sites of photosynthesis within the leaf, from intense bright light that would otherwise cause them irreparable damage. Thus, anthocyanins effectively function as plant sunscreens.

Secondly, they are among the impressive numbers of chemicals that defend against herbivory. In some cases, the anthocyanin pigments themselves may make leaves unpalatable to would-be predators, or it might be just that their coloration makes the leaves look less appealing as a meal. The darker shades of anthocyanin-rich leaves make them less distinguishable against shadowy forest backdrops. The leaves are thus simply not seen by those in search of a fresh spring salad.

Of course, plant pressures differ markedly across regions, and this perhaps explains why the Chinese tulip tree displays more vibrant anthocyanin-derived spring coloration compared with its Western Hemisphere counterpart. But that is not to say that the North American tulip tree doesn't produce those pigments; it does, but to a lesser degree. The American species is evidently able to invest its early-season attentions elsewhere more swiftly, to get on with the business of producing the all-important chlorophyll to maximise its photosynthetic potential.

Besides spring coloration, another difference between the leaves of the Chinese and North American tulip trees is revealed by their undersides. Flipping the leaves reveals a difference in colour – pale green in the American tulip tree, nearly blue in the Chinese species – but to see the reason for this difference requires a hand lens or similar magnification. Close inspection reveals that the leaf-backs of the Chinese tulip tree are covered in tiny, densely set papillae – nipple-shaped projections derived from the outermost layer of leaf cells – which are coated with a layer of wax, giving the surface its distinctive bluish sheen. Papillae are far from exclusive to the Chinese tulip tree. They are often present in drought-adapted, xerophytic plants, providing protection against excessive sunlight and helping to reduce water loss by contributing to boundary layer functions that are otherwise performed by surface hairs in other plant species. But papillae also provide self-drying and self-cleaning services to the leaf surface.

How do they do this? Being so densely set means that there are only minuscule depressions between the papillae, in which there is a very thin layer of air. Due to the surface tension of water – i.e. the tendency of water droplets to bead up – water drips quickly off the surface, rather than penetrating the tiny gaps, thus providing the leaf with an impressive self-drying mechanism. And as for why this is useful, the reason is simple enough: removing potentially dirty, microbe-ridden water helps to keep the leaves disease-free.

This hydrophobicity – being difficult to wet – is known as the 'lotus effect', as the same water-repelling mechanism is employed by the leaves of lotus flower (*Nelumbo*) species. The self-cleaning aspects of this phenomenon are being replicated in synthetic products from paints to roofing tiles and clothes, and its utility continues to be explored.

So then, why might the Chinese tulip tree have developed this wonderful water-repelling method, yet the North American tulip tree has not? It comes back to those environmental pressures again. For a tulip tree in the forests of eastern North America, the volume of rain it experiences doesn't warrant a specific mechanism to avoid staying soaked, whereas the wilds of southern China and northern Vietnam are subject to near constant, monsoonal summer rains. So, it pays to look closely at trees, especially those that forecast the weather.

SUGAR MAPLE

Acer saccharum

The forests of eastern North America are renowned for diverse species assemblages that exhibit show-stopping autumn colour. Vibrant yellows, reds and oranges from trees including oaks (*Quercus*), sweet gum (*Liquidambar styraciflua*), tupelo (*Nyssa sylvatica*) and other maples light up the scene in a glorious month-long seasonal finale. As nights cool and the days become shorter, deciduous trees prepare for colder weather by shutting down and shedding their leaves, though not before the annual colour party, with sugar maple its headline act.

Native to a large part of eastern North America, from southern Canada to as far south as Georgia in the United States, sugar maple belongs to a 'species complex' which contains half a dozen or so closely related, but mostly ill-defined, species. Maples occur in nearly all temperate regions in the Northern Hemisphere, and are at their most diverse in eastern Asia. A single maple species, *Acer laurinum*, reaches the Southern Hemisphere, where it grows in tropical forests in Indonesia.

Sugar maple is a large tree, with five-lobed, broadly palmate leaves. For many it has come to represent the genus, though the variety of leaf shapes and sizes is much more diverse among maples than many would expect. The largest leaves, typically a foot across but occasionally even double that, belong to the western North American *Acer macrophyllum*, aptly known as bigleaf maple, with a classically hand-shaped leaf with broad lobes, while the leaves of the Chinese Faber's maple (*A. fabri*) can have tiny leaves, only a few centimetres long, without a lobe in sight. There are even maples with compound leaves. Box elder (*Acer negundo*), another North American species, displays pinnately compound foliage. In fact, the most recognisable unifying character of maple species is not their leaves but their paired, winged fruits, often referred to as 'helicopters', which break apart and spin in the air as they are blown from tree to ground in autumn.

Several maples are renowned for their autumn colour, with the sugar maples among the most celebrated. Typically, they turn fiery hues of orange, though shades from yellow to red are also common. And each autumn, as these charismatic trees prepare for winter, thousands of 'leaf peepers' flock to the best stands in Canada and the United States to witness the spectacle.

Autumn colour is highly variable among deciduous trees throughout the temperate world. Some trees exhibit virtually no colour, while others produce outstanding colour as an exception rather than the rule. Sugar maple and its fellow eastern North American associates are as reliable as they come.

Autumn colour is in no small part a side effect of the physiological processes that have taken place in the leaves long before the autumn. Throughout spring and summer, foliage and young stems act as the tree's food factories. In them, there is an abundance of the green pigment chlorophyll, which is responsible for converting the sun's energy via photosynthesis into chemical energy for the plant's growth and development. Also present at this time are other pigments, but they are usually entirely masked by the wealth of chlorophyll. The presence of pigments in the leaves is the result of a variety of metabolic processes including photosynthesis, and while continuously produced, they are also constantly being used up. In autumn, shortening days trigger thickenings in the leaf veins, which slows the flow of water. Photosynthesis starts to decline and with it, the production of chlorophyll. Gradually, as the remaining chlorophyll breaks down, the yellows and oranges that contribute to the plant's autumn finery are revealed. The pigments that provide these colours, xanthophylls and carotenes, are slower to break down than chlorophyll. They belong to a group of pigments called carotenoids – the same ones that give carrots their orange coloration.

At the same time, when about half of the chlorophyll content has been lost, another set of pigments – anthocyanins – begin to be produced, and these provide the reds and purple shades that are seen in a great many species. Black maple (*Acer nigrum* or *A. saccharum* subsp. *nigrum*), a close relative of the sugar maple, can be readily distinguished by the presence of xanthophylls and relative absence of anthocyanins in the leaves, for example. Black maple leaves only ever turn yellow or pale orange, whereas those of many other maples, along with tupelos and sweetgums, exhibit the darker shades associated with anthocyanin production.

The production of anthocyanins relies on the breakdown of sugars already present in the leaves and – importantly – on the presence of long periods of bright sunlight. Other factors are also required, but in general, sunny days and cool but not freezing nights are needed for the development of the darker pigments. These conditions are more commonly experienced in eastern North America and in parts of eastern Asia, such as in Japan and Korea, which goes some way to explaining why the seasonal show is often better in those places than in western Europe and parts of western North America.

As to why anthocyanins are produced in autumn, the consensus of scientific opinion is that they somehow protect the photosynthetic apparatus from bright light while it is being disassembled. Ideally, all of the remaining nutrients, amino acids and proteins in the leaves would be transferred into the stems and roots for the winter to be recycled in the spring.

The colour show ends when the leaves fall off, of course, but this, too, is a complex business. At the base of the leaf where its stem, the petiole, attaches to the twig, is an abscission (or separation) zone. With the onset of autumn, cells on either side of the zone divide, producing new cells that are rich in lignin and suberin (wood and cork) and these compounds both weaken the connection between the leaf and the rest of the tree and help to form a waterproof layer for the area once the leaves abscise (detach). Eventually, the leaves are blown off by wind, forced off by frost or fall of their own accord.

Like all kinds of maples, sugar maples are widely cultivated outside of their native territory, though for the reasons explained above, expecting autumn colour anything like on their home ground is usually a disappointment. Occasionally, the conditions in another region come together to produce a glorious spectacle, but these instances are mostly short-lived. For more reliable autumn colour, gardeners have better luck with the hundreds of horticultural selections of Japanese maples (*Acer palmatum* and its relatives). Anthocyanin production does seem less fickle with the Asian maples, and many cultivars produce vivid dark reds regardless of the weather. And just as people flock to the forests of eastern North America, they do the same in Japan, where observance of the spectacle among the native maples is known as *momijigari*.

So locally significant is the sugar maple that it has been designated as the state tree of no fewer than five US states and its leaf adorns the Canadian national flag, an emblem of the country's intimate relationship with the species across both French and English Canada. For as well as spectacular seasonal colour, the sugar maple is also the primary source of maple syrup. Trees are tapped in early spring before their buds swell, with around 36 litres of sap needed for every litre of syrup. Almost any maple can be tapped, but the highest sugar concentration is in sugar maple and its close relative, black maple.

Indigenous people in North America's eastern woodlands knew to tap these trees for the sweet sap, and the practice was adopted by European settlers. Of great economic significance to Canada, the sugar maple leaf is featured extensively on both its printed and minted money, and the leaves appear on many versions of its collectable gold bullion coins. However, botanical purists have a history of being upset with the Canadian Mint. The front face of the Canadian copper penny (in circulation from 1937 until 2013, when it was discontinued), for example, showed a pair of sugar maple leaves alternately arranged on a branch (maple leaves are always oppositely arranged). The $20, $50 and $100 banknotes are a problem too. The stylised maple leaf image that appears on modern polymer notes as a small, silver-rimmed transparent watermark – one of numerous security features – has been roundly criticised for bearing a closer resemblance to the European Norway maple (*Acer platanoides*) than to sugar maple. The two species are often confused but are easily distinguished by the sap in their leaf stalks, which in sugar maple runs clear and in the Norway maple is milky white.

As well as finding its way onto Canadian currency, Norway maple has also infiltrated many eastern North American forests and has become aggressively invasive to the degree that it threatens to displace sugar maple in parts of its natural habitat. Other than this, there are few threats to sugar maple in the wild and scientists consider it a highly adaptable species that will probably cope well with warming temperatures. Maple syrup production may decline when the spring comes early, but autumn colour won't diminish even a shade as long as the sun shines.

BLACK WALNUT

Juglans nigra

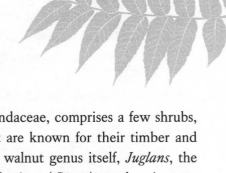

The walnut family, Juglandaceae, comprises a few shrubs, but primarily trees that are known for their timber and edible nuts. As well as the walnut genus itself, *Juglans*, the family includes the hickories (*Carya*) and wingnuts (*Pterocarya*), as well as a few smaller genera that together occur in temperate and tropical parts of the Americas and eastern Asia. Along with the hickories, the walnuts belong to one of only a small number of tree genera that occur in both North America and China, but are more speciose in the Americas.

Like all members of its family, walnut leaves are pinnately compound, with numerous leaflets that vary in shape depending on species. Total leaf size is often very large. As with members of the pea family, Fabaceae, and other pinnate-leaved trees, the annual growth of a long leaf stem on which to hold their leaflets appears to be a more economical investment than growing more wood on which to support simple, undivided leaves.

All walnut leaves have broad petiole bases, which – when the leaves fall in autumn – leave a 'monkey-faced' scar on the stem, formed by the traces of vascular connections between leaf and stem. Walnuts stems have a chambered pith, easily observed by cutting a twig longitudinally with a sharp blade. The regular segmentations are reminiscent of an upturned woodlouse – though without the flailing legs. Walnuts share this pith character with the related wingnuts, whose most obvious difference is, predictably, the winged fruit. The pith colour of the various walnut species, in combination with leaf and fruiting characters, can help to differentiate them one from another.

Black walnut, from the forests of eastern North America, is one of the most familiar of the walnuts and, like other members of the family, its leaves are wonderfully fragrant when gently rubbed, the scent released from aromatic glands that clothe the leaf surface. Often over half a metre in length, the leaves have slightly curved, finely serrated leaflets that droop either side of the leaf stem and usually lack a terminal leaflet. Their fruity aroma is also a feature of the husk of its fruit, the seed of which is a source of commercial walnuts, though those of the so-called common, or English, walnut are more used. That species, though cultivated in Britain since Roman times, is not actually native to Europe. It is thought to be native to western and central Asia, though its true range is virtually untraceable, given the degree to which it has been spread both intentionally and otherwise, such is the value of its fruit. Walnuts are a favourite of squirrels – as well as humans – and these rodents have proven highly efficient walnut propagators, with forgotten nut caches developing into saplings that emerge in unexpected places.

In many areas, black walnut leaves are relatively pest-free and remain in good condition all summer long, before turning beautiful shades of yellow in autumn. They drop early, usually before other trees have started with the annual colour show. Walnuts play host to a number of species of aphids and scale insects that preferentially suck sap and then excrete the waste on the leaves or the ground below. The sticky, sugar-rich liquid is known as honeydew. This is generally most noticed by people who have parked their car beneath walnut trees, only to return to find a sticky coating across the roof of their vehicle. However, walnuts are far from the only trees that 'produce' honeydew from their leaves. In temperate areas several maples (*Acer*), birches (*Betula*) and limes (*Tilia*) also harbour prolific honeydew producers. Tree identification skills pay off when attempting to park in treed municipal car parks!

All walnuts, but particularly black walnut, are also renowned for their allelopathic qualities. Allelopathy is the production and release by plants of chemical substances, known as allelochemicals, that inhibit the growth of other neighbouring plants. Allelochemical release may occur in several ways, for example, when parts of the plant decompose, or via leaching, volatilisation or root exudation. The allelopathic effect is often a result of a complex interaction between multiple chemical compounds, with the resulting mixtures slowing – or even halting – the growth of those competing for the same resources.

In walnuts, the allelopathic effect has long been attributed to the chemical juglone, which is present in the leaves, leaf buds and all growing parts of the tree. Juglone inhibits respiration in plants, with vegetables including tomatoes, peppers and potatoes all highly susceptible (these are all members of the nightshade family, Solanaceae). Black walnut and butternut (*Juglans cinerea*), its fellow eastern North American relative, are known to be prolific juglone producers, releasing it in herbicidal concentrations. Exposure to juglone can kill some plants, though several species are also tolerant and grow close to walnuts without any ill effects.

Juglone is found in its highest volumes in the walnut fruit, which never falls far from the tree, thus heavily toxifying the area immediately beneath it. However, the chemical is not particularly persistent in the soil, so growing plants on former walnut tree sites is seldom much of a problem. Other plants, including fellow members of the walnut family, also produce juglone, but in lesser concentrations and usually in quantities that do not have a growth-inhibiting effect. The allelopathic nature of black walnut has in some cases been used to the benefit of tree growers, with commercial orchards growing other species of walnut choosing to graft their trees onto black walnut rootstocks to conveniently eliminate competition.

As well as having a toxic effect on other plants, black walnut can also be problematic for animals. Horses bedded on walnut woodchips or sawdust – or even in stables located within the proximity of walnut trees – can contract acute laminitis, i.e. severe inflammation of the foot that can cause permanent damage. However, the cause of this is in fact not juglone, although the responsible compound is as yet unknown. Decomposing walnut husks too can be poisonous to livestock if consumed, and potentially fatal to dogs. Again, the key chemical at play here is not considered to be juglone but a toxin produced by a *Penicillium* mould fungus, which is a natural part of the decomposition process. This fungus can penetrate the fruit itself and so as good as a good walnut can be, anything showing signs of rot is best avoided.

Black walnut timber is considered to be of the highest grade, and is widely used for furniture, musical instruments and interior design components. So sought-after is its wood that nearly all the best wild black walnut trees have long since been harvested; entire trees have even been stolen right out of the ground. Regrettably, the effects of juglone and black walnut's other toxins are not enough to put off these tree thieves.

COMMON BEECH

Fagus sylvatica

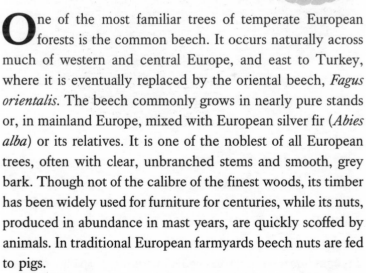

One of the most familiar trees of temperate European forests is the common beech. It occurs naturally across much of western and central Europe, and east to Turkey, where it is eventually replaced by the oriental beech, *Fagus orientalis*. The beech commonly grows in nearly pure stands or, in mainland Europe, mixed with European silver fir (*Abies alba*) or its relatives. It is one of the noblest of all European trees, often with clear, unbranched stems and smooth, grey bark. Though not of the calibre of the finest woods, its timber has been widely used for furniture for centuries, while its nuts, produced in abundance in mast years, are quickly scoffed by animals. In traditional European farmyards beech nuts are fed to pigs.

With fewer than a dozen species, *Fagus* is one of the smaller genera in the beech family, Fagaceae, a family dominated by the oaks (*Quercus*) and stone oaks (*Lithocarpus*), which have over 750 species between them. While several shrubs occur elsewhere in the beech family, all beeches are trees, and outside of woodland settings, specimens develop broad, stately crowns, frequently supported by sprawling buttress roots. Despite the additional assistance, mature trees are prone to windthrow, with full canopies often belying rotting, hidden root systems. Beech trees are capable of living for a more-than-respectable 250 years-plus, though they don't have quite the longevity of some of their beech family relatives, such as the European oaks, which are renowned for their continued robustness over many centuries.

The leaves of common beech are distinctive: glossy, dark green above and lighter below, elliptic in outline, with regularly spaced veins either side of a prominent midrib. The margins are wavy and fringed with wispy hairs. Famously shade-adapted – *sylvatica* means 'of the forest' – beech trees cast a shade so dense that little apart from seedling beeches grow beneath them. Early in the spring, however, as the days begin to lengthen and more heat is felt in the sun, there appear wild carpets of wood anemone (*Anemonoides nemorosa*) and bluebell (*Hyacinthoides non-scripta*) among the column-like trunks.

These cyclical changes dictate when the trees of temperate forests spring into action. To protect new leaves from frost, new growth commences in response to environmental triggers that indicate that spring is on the way. For some trees, flowering or leafing out will be initiated only after a number of daylight hours has been exceeded, while other species respond primarily to sustained changes in temperature. Common beech has evolved exacting mechanisms that regulate winter dormancy and to ensure that leaves do not emerge and expand when there is still a high likelihood of damaging frost. The last thing a tree wants – evolutionarily speaking – is to expend energy to form overwintering buds, only to have the new leaves and all the potential growth they represent cut down in a few freezing moments. A changing climate, with increasingly erratic and unpredictable 'seasonal' events, is likely to wreak havoc with a tree's internal programming.

With dense crowns, packed with leaves, a mature beech can sequester, or 'fix', around 2 kilograms of carbon dioxide every hour in daylight, at the same time emitting enough oxygen for about ten people a year. If anyone ever needed reminding of the value of trees, we could point them towards the nearest beech.

For a large tree, having the capacity to grow in a shaded environment is a serious advantage. To do so, broadleaved trees frequently produce both 'sun leaves' and 'shade leaves'. In common beech, shade leaves are around 30 per cent larger than sun leaves. These provide a larger area for absorbing light energy for photosynthesis where light levels are low. The smaller sun leaves have a reduced surface area to limit water loss through transpiration. They are thicker too, packed with more chloroplasts, to allow for increased rates of photosynthesis. From the top of the tree towards the base, leaf thickness decreases.

Common beech trees are most prominent in the landscape in autumn, their leaves turning shades of gold and russet brown, with hillside stands recognisable from miles away. As throughout the growing season, once fallen the leaves play a key role in the maintenance of the forest floor. Largely unpalatable to earthworms, they decay slowly, and in doing so create a deep layer of organic matter, which keeps the soil from drying out, but also supports a wide variety of organisms and their interactions. As they break down, the leaves return nutrients, most crucially nitrogen, to the soil, which are then recycled and taken up by the roots. Beech trees are exceptional 'soil improvers' in this respect.

Common beech is also a hugely popular choice in urban parks and gardens. Numerous horticultural forms are cultivated, with great variation in traits of leaf shape, size and colour. These variations are mostly 'sports' – one-off mutations arising on single branches. In some cases, a seedling may carry an appealing mutation throughout all of its tissues. For centuries, variants have been selected from trees and propagated by grafting. There are several 'cut-leaved' beeches, with deeply dissected leaves, and a number with white- or pink-variegated leaves. Most frequent are the copper and purple-leaved beeches. In these, the green pigment in the leaves, chlorophyll, is masked by anthocyanins, which vary in amount and make trees with leaves that can range from bronze to deep red, or even purplish-black. In most cases the darkest leaves are those most exposed to the sun, while shaded leaves, appearing within the crown, are paler.

Beech leaves on non-reproductive shoots are often retained dead on the branch until pushed off by spring growth. A number of plants in the oak family are prone to this – a phenomenon known as marcescence. Marcescence is a feature of primarily non-reproductive shoots, thought to afford a degree of protection to the overwintering buds by reducing air flow around the stems. This phenomenon is also commonly seen on sheared beeches used for hedging, which is perhaps the most common use for beech trees. The world's longest and tallest maintained hedge is a beech hedge running along a roadside in Perthshire, Scotland, which measures over 500 metres in length and around 30 metres in height.

Though earthworms don't favour fallen beech leaves, the tender, young ones are popular with foragers as fresh additions to salads or fried to make beech leaf chips. They are also used to make 'beech leaf noyau', a sweetened, gin-based liqueur, whose origins reputedly trace back to the chair-making trade in southern England's Chiltern hills in the eighteenth and nineteenth centuries. Another by-product of a valuable and versatile tree.

NEEM

Azadirachta indica

Neem may be the most useful of tropical trees. In scientific publications it is often referred to as a multipurpose tree. And no wonder – neem provides a multitude of practical products, from biopesticides to toothpaste and from animal feed to medicines and nectar for honey.

Neem belongs to the mahogany family, Meliaceae, a tropical assemblage that includes trees known for their valuable timbers, and neem wood is certainly widely used as it is both hard and resistant to termites, borers and fungi. It is highly valued as fuel wood and makes good charcoal. Unlike the mahoganies of commerce, neem is rough-grained and does not finish well, so is considered more of an industrial wood, and unsuitable for furniture; though in India, neem wood is commonly used for the carving of temple idols.

As ornamental trees go, neem is valued for its rapid growth, strong branching and attractive, rounded crown, as well as the rough, reddish-brown, fissured and flaking bark that develops on mature individuals. The name *Azadirachta* is from the Persian *azad darakht*, which means 'noble tree'. Like most mahogany relatives, neem bears small, sweetly fragrant, nectar-rich flowers in large, drooping panicles. Bees are wildly attracted to the flowers, and the honey they produce is excellent. The flowers are soon followed by small, yellow, inflated fruits, and a tree in fruit looks like it is dotted with popcorn. The leaves are dark green, pinnately compound, and consist of numerous toothed and pointed, curved leaflets on a slender rachis (the leaf stalk above the petiole on a pinnately compound leaf). Apply a little imagination and each pair of leaflets resembles a bird in flight and the whole leaf a row of birds on a wire, about to lift off simultaneously. Although evergreen in areas with consistent rainfall, neem can drop its leaves and become dormant in arid climes when moisture is wanting. This opportunistic deciduous behaviour is a valuable adaption for surviving both regular dry spells and more severe droughts; the dropping of a canopy full of leaves for many tropical evergreens would indicate the point of no return and a rapid descent into the land of the dead.

Neem's deep roots give it considerable resilience with respect to drought, and the usually evergreen foliage and broad spreading crown make it an attractive choice both as a shade tree and for afforestation (the conversion of non-forested land to forest). Indeed, neem is a much-exploited species in sub-Saharan Africa for combatting desertification. Neem has the ability to grow in a wide variety of soil types, even salt-contaminated soils, and because of its deep roots, it does not compete with crops for shallow moisture. Another advantage of neem for farmers is that the leaves are useful as fodder for livestock, particularly goats and camels (two animals, it must be said, that are capable of eating almost anything), as well as for mulching and green manures. Adding to the list – and maybe the most important of its valuable qualities – is its amazing resistance to pests.

Farmers across south Asia where *Azadirachta indica* is native have known for millennia that this tree has remarkable properties, including its ability to repel arthropod pests, but they also knew that neem was effective in taking care of pests that attacked other plants. Neem oil (also known as margosa oil), which is produced by crushing neem seeds, is used widely as a biopesticide. It is known to check a range of disease-causing fungi and bacteria and is estimated to control some 200 species of arthropod pests.

The active ingredient in neem oil is azadirachtin, a now well-studied anti-feedant and growth disruptor. As most students of the natural world know, insects and other arthropod pests have rigid exoskeletons that encase their soft bodies, and as they grow they need to moult periodically; that is, shed their exoskeleton and produce a new, larger one that can accommodate an increased body size. Internal hormones determine the timing of these body changes in arthropods, and azadirachtin effectively disrupts these hormones, meaning that the normal moulting process cannot take place. This usually results in an inability of the pest to reach sexual maturity and produce eggs, and generally causes premature death. Luckily, azadirachtin is considered to have low toxicity for mammals and thus can be used in stored grains and around people, where pesticides would normally be dangerous.

Other parts of the neem tree contain compounds related to azadirachtin that can also be used against microbes and arthropod pests. For example, the dried leaves are often mixed with stored seed to prevent predation, and the tree's antiseptic resin is added to toothpaste, soap and lotions. Across the Indian subcontinent, neem 'chew sticks' are routinely used as tooth cleaners and to freshen breath, presumably through their antibacterial action.

Neem is widely used in folk medicine. The bark and leaves are commonly used to treat skin conditions, including relieving the symptoms of leprosy, and the flowers are used for their tonic effects, the fruits for their laxative properties and for softening skin, and the root bark to treat fever and nausea. While legitimate clinical trials to support claims are slow in coming, there is evidence that many traditional and some novel applications (as a spermicide, for example) have yielded both positive and reproducible results. It's little wonder, then, that neem is a popular tree that continues to be planted across the tropical world.

In an increasing number of habitats, however, neem has escaped cultivation and invaded wild lands where it is not native. As a result, neem is now considered an invasive species on several Caribbean islands, in west Africa and in northern Australia. Despite its invasive potential, neem plantations are still common. Probably the largest, with 50,000 trees, was begun in the 1980s on the Plains of Arafat in Saudi Arabia. The plantation was intended to provide shade for Muslim haj pilgrims (the site is close to Mecca) and to commemorate the Prophet Mohammad's *Khutbatul-Wada* (farewell sermon), which is said to have been delivered to the faithful in the year 632 CE from nearby Mount Arafat.

SHAPE-SHIFTERS

The tree which moves some to tears of joy is in
the eyes of others only a green thing that stands in the
way. Some see nature all ridicule and deformity . . .
and some scarce see nature at all. But to the eyes of
the man of imagination, nature is imagination itself.

WILLIAM BLAKE

*From seeds, mighty trees grow (to misquote the famous fourteenth-century English proverb: 'Mighty oaks from little acorns grow'),
but plants usually pass through definite stages before they can get
there, and this is often expressed in the leaves. Heterophylly is the
general term for this (hetero = different + phylly = leaves) and
most frequently this phenomenon describes changes from distinctive
juvenile to different-looking reproductively mature growth, and is
usually manifested in changes to leaf shape, size or arrangement.
A common form of heterophylly is the gain or loss of leaf armature
– holm oak and common holly are examples of this. Not all plants
change the shape of their leaves, let alone add spines, and in many
the changes are barely detectable, but some changes are huge. Leaf
changes in New Zealand lancewood are, as you will see, enough to
confuse a flightless bird. Heterophylly in Tasmanian blue gum is
somewhat less extreme, though there are wholesale changes to both
leaf shape and their arrangement on the stems. And though like the
blue gum, sassafras is most famous for its aroma (it smells of root
beer), it's also known to change from one- to two- or three-lobed
leaves, depending on the weather. Plants do not stand still.*

TASMANIAN BLUE GUM

Eucalyptus globulus

Eucalypts are iconic trees. With over 900 species, they comprise the *Eucalyptus* genus and two smaller genera, *Angophora* and *Corymbia*, and though a small number of species occur in New Guinea, Indonesia and the Philippines, they are mainly associated with Australia. And justly so, as eucalypt forest makes up more than three-quarters of all Australian forest, covering more than 100 million hectares.

Though some eucalypts can be shrubby, many are most definitely trees. Indeed, the world's tallest flowering plant is a eucalypt: *Eucalyptus regnans*, the swamp or stringy gum, which is sometimes called mountain ash (and is not to be confused with members of the *Sorbus* genus or the true ashes in the genus *Fraxinus*). It is native to Tasmania and Victoria and is known to grow to nearly 100 metres, while legend has it that at least one example topped 130 metres. That would make it the tallest-growing of all trees, though current tall tree records are held by conifers, with a specimen of the Californian coast redwood (*Sequoia sempervirens*), known as Hyperion, measuring just shy of 116 metres in 2017.

Eucalypts are vigorous growers and have excellent wood properties. Unsurprisingly then, they are valued as timber trees both within and far beyond their native climes. Highly adaptable, their success across regions has led to an over-reliance on them and they have become the world's most widely planted hardwood trees. Both voracious water consumers and drought-tolerant, eucalypts often extract water at considerable depth, lowering water tables beyond the reach of native trees. Concerted action is now required to restore habitats across several continents and reset balances within fragile ecological communities.

The leaves of most eucalypts are evergreen, silvery-blue to green and fragrant, with a camphor-like scent. In maturity they are alternately arranged, lance-shaped and often slightly curved. Endemic to south-eastern Australia, Tasmanian blue gum has some of the longest leaves of all eucalypts, extending to up to 30 centimetres in length. Eucalypt leaves often hang vertically, or nearly so, as a means of keeping cool while continuing to photosynthesise. This means that they offer little in the way of shade, and consequently some eucalypt forests are known as shadeless forests.

The leaves of young trees, however, are often very different. Eucalypts are one of the trees most clearly displaying the phenomenon of leaf dimorphism or heterophylly. Juvenile leaves are usually arranged oppositely and are rounded, held stiffly, clasping the stems, rather than drooping down from slender petioles.

In their juvenile form, *Eucalyptus* leaves are a favourite among florists, having gained popularity in Europe and North America in the 1980s. More recently, they have found favour with interior plant enthusiasts, for whom the cut, dried stems are an aesthetic choice. Their popularity is fierce enough to rival the fiddle-leaf fig (*Ficus lyrata*), while their fresh camphor scent is also an attraction for some. The young leaves and stems are silvery-grey to bluish-green, with this attractive coloration being due to the presence of a waxy bloom.

As well as possessing ornamental qualities (and living plants may also be pruned for this same effect), this glaucousness, produced in varying amounts among *Eucalyptus* species, is also associated with frost resistance, as the higher in altitude the trees grow, the thicker the waxes and more glaucous their leaves become. And though unproven as to whether by luck or design, these foliar waxes have also been shown to form a physical barrier to the eucalyptus tortoise beetle (*Paropsis charybdis*), a leaf-eater attracted to the leaves of several *Eucalyptus* species. The waxes are slippery to the beetle and prevent them from getting a grip on the leaves, thus rendering them unable to be eaten. Juvenile leaves occur not only on young plants, but also in response to damage, including defoliation, so the waxes present on new, juvenile growth serve to protect the tree while its energy reserves are being used to support its recovery.

Though dominant in Australian forests, very few animals favour eucalypt leaves as food. This is due to the highly effective chemical defences of the leaves, which are packed with essential oils; toxic molecules that render them poisonous to most mammals (as well as giving them their distinctive scent). The leaves contain mostly fibre, but little protein, making them nutrient-poor, though the leaves are tolerated in moderation by some marsupials and are the main food source of koalas.

Having co-evolved with eucalypts, koalas are able to efficiently flush eucalyptus toxins from their systems. Thus, they can chew through vast amounts without becoming sick. They need to eat significant amounts of leaves to sustain themselves, between 500 to 800 grams daily, which is more than three times the amount that would be fatal to humans and other mammals. Perhaps it is unsurprising then that koalas have little in the way of competition for their food. (They manage to squeeze their consumption into just a few hours too, as they sleep between 20 and 22 hours each day.)

With this unique capacity, koalas are then absolute specialist folivores; and they don't eat just any eucalyptus either. They are highly selective and have the ability to sniff out the best leaves, which are those richest in monoterpenes, the compounds that are a key component of the essential oils. Eucalyptus leaves are relatively low in nutrients, but koalas' slow metabolism means that they are able to extract sufficient energy as well as all their moisture needs from these leaves alone. The Tasmanian blue gum is one of the species favoured by koalas, though their diet varies region to region across Australia, as they take advantage of the best available leaves in their locality.

In parts of their range, where populations have been high, koalas have been known to defoliate entire *Eucalyptus* forests. This inevitably becomes a problem as outstripping the food supply leaves koalas at risk of starvation, and in areas where the animals are reliant on isolated pockets of eucalypt forest and are unable to move safely to other areas this is a particular concern. As a result, koalas have attracted the attention of conservation authorities and the species is now listed as Vulnerable on the International Union for Conservation of Nature (IUCN) Red List.

The essential oils secreted from eucalyptus leaves are, unsurprisingly, the source of eucalyptus oil. Over 300 species of eucalyptus are known to possess essential oils, though less than 10 per cent of that number have been commercially exploited for it and around half a dozen make up the bulk of eucalyptus oil produced globally. Oil from Tasmanian blue gum, which is the most common source, is produced in China, India, Spain, South Africa and across parts of South America. The oil-producing glands are generally visible as tiny dots on the leaf surface, and their various shapes, sizes and placement are sometimes used to aid species identification. They are well worth a closer look.

Eucalyptus oil is extracted via a process of steam distillation, whereby dry steam is passed through the plant material to release the volatile compounds within. The expressed vapour is then condensed and collected. Eucalyptus essential oil has myriad uses, the most significant being for medicinal purposes, and the oils that are richest in cineole, an aromatic compound valued as an anti-inflammatory, are the most sought-after.

Although eucalyptus oil was first commercialised in Australia in the mid-nineteenth century, Aboriginal Australians have known of its medicinal properties for millennia. They established several uses for the leaves, including restorative therapy beds that used leaves laid over piping hot coals to give off healing steam to treat aching bodies resting above. Other uses for the oil include soaps and perfumes, insect repellents and pesticides, and its properties as an antimicrobial have also led to it being used in household cleaning products and mouthwashes.

This is a book about leaves, but you can't talk about eucalypts without mentioning the bark. Some species have vibrantly coloured bark, including most famously *Eucalpytus deglupta*, which is colourful enough to be known as the rainbow eucalyptus. It is also the only eucalypt to occur in the Northern Hemisphere and one of only a handful that don't grow naturally in Australia at all. In many species, eucalyptus bark peels in huge sheets that hang from branches before eventually falling. And it doesn't do that for nothing. Periodic fires are a natural part of eucalyptus forest ecology as the oils present in the leaves render them highly combustible, while the bark contributes to the flammable litter layer, and both burn quickly. The resultant heat opens seed capsules held on branches, and the seeds drop to the cleared, nutrient-rich soil to begin the next generation. Adult eucalypts are resilient though and, after fire, branches bearing new leaves resprout from dormant buds found below the bark, allowing them to recover and continue their role in the forest.

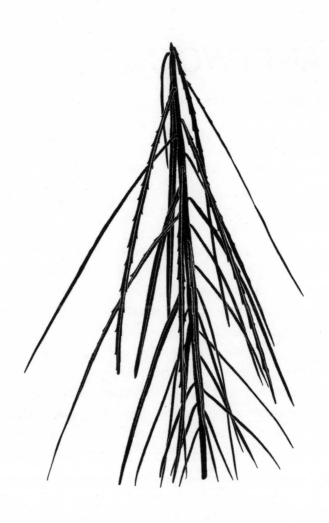

LANCEWOOD

Pseudopanax crassifolius

While the ginseng family, Araliaceae, features plants with spectacularly large leaves, such as the many-leafleted scheffleras (see page 289), it also includes species that, while markedly different in foliar characters, are also highly architectural and no less intriguing.

Among the most striking in any setting, and most fascinating from an evolutionary perspective, are the lancewood (*Pseudopanax crassifolius*) and the toothed lancewood (*P. ferox*). The *Pseudopanax* genus once included species from Chile, New Caledonia, New Zealand and Tasmania; now, though, following reclassification, it comprises seven species, all endemic to New Zealand and neighbouring islands.

The vernacular name lancewood is thought to derive from the way its wood splits into lance-like shards, or perhaps from the Māori use of the juvenile tree stems as lances to spear *kereru*, the New Zealand wood pigeon (*Hemiphaga novaeseelandiae*). To the Māori, all *Pseudopanax* species are known as horoeka.

Like the eucalypts, lancewoods are notably heterophyllous, with distinct leaf forms produced at different life stages. This is perhaps most marked in *Pseudopanax crassifolius*, which has four discrete leaf forms. As a seedling, its leaves are small, more or less oblong and tapered at the base, with tough, stout teeth or even small lobes; then – and most extraordinarily – once the plant develops a straight, single stem, it holds leaves only on the uppermost parts, with these being up to a metre long and angled steeply downward. At this point these are stiff, leathery, almost sword-shaped leaves, with margins armed with evenly spaced, hardened, sharp teeth. Later, as the tree begins to produce branches, the leaves take on a more ascending posture. Some of the leaves are divided into three or even five leaflets, while others retain the characters of the previous stage, though not the extraordinary length. In some cases, this stage – the third – is skipped entirely. In the final, mature stage, the leaves become undivided again. They are narrow and up to around 20 centimetres long, tapering at the base to a stout petiole, while the margins are largely toothless other than towards the tip. Only at this point does the tree begin to produce flowers, the males and females occurring on separate trees. The entire process – from juvenile seedling to reproductively mature tree – usually takes around 15 to 20 years. Trees can ultimately attain a modest height of 15 metres, and they eventually develop smooth bark, it being somewhat more prominently ridged in youth.

It is for the curious juvenile foliage that lancewood is most well-known; in the horticultural trade, the tree is marketed on its distinctive 'weird' look. So different are the juvenile leaves of *Pseudopanax crassifolius* from those of an adult plant that the two were once thought to be from separate species. It wasn't until many years after specimens were first collected by European explorers, who gathered separate specimens of both juvenile and adult forms, that botanists realised that both came from the same tree. Though trees with two or more distinct types of leaves are common in – even characteristic of – the New Zealand flora, no species displays quite such diversity as the lancewood.

The question of why lancewood and other New Zealand natives present such contrasting leaf forms is a popular one, but answering it isn't straightforward because the species that could offer proof of the most likely theory is long since extinct.

Polynesians arrived in New Zealand around 700 years ago, some 300 years before Europeans first landed there. Prior to the arrival of Europeans, New Zealand had no browsing or grazing mammals; originally that ecological niche was filled by large flightless birds known as moas. Moas comprised nine species, the largest of which grew 3 metres tall and weighed nearly a quarter of a ton; though within 100 years of human habitation in New Zealand all moas had been hunted to extinction. Although they are thought never to have been very common, moas are considered to have been the dominant browsers of foliage from ground level to around 3 metres, across all landscapes in New Zealand, and lancewood is thought to have evolved mechanisms to deter moas from eating it.

The most obvious of these is the transition from juvenile to adult foliage, which happens to occur once the tree reaches around 3 metres tall – that is, once it is out of reach of the moa. Before it gets there, though, it has needed to protect itself through the seedling, juvenile and intermediate stages, employing multiple, sometimes elaborate mechanisms. The first comes at the seedling stage, when the young leaves of lancewood are mottled, with irregular blotching across the leaf surface. Such mottling tends to break up the outlines of leaves, and it has been theorised that this would have made it difficult for moas to pick out the leaves against a background of leaf litter. Furthermore, the leaves at this stage are dark green to purple-brown, resembling dead or dying leaves rather than fresh ones and therefore less appealing to a herbivore.

The barb-like teeth on the leaf margins are also prominently highlighted with bright spots around about them, probably as a warning to the moa that the leaves would make a difficult meal. This phenomenon of aposematic colouration – advertising to potential predators that they are not worth eating – is common in animals (think brightly coloured poison-dart frogs) and in plants. The mottling and brightly coloured teeth exhibited by lancewood are both illustrations of this phenomenon.

The bright spots around the teeth of lancewood themselves are a result of increased anthocyanin levels in this part of the leaf and, as they are so sharp and tough, to attempt to eat the leaves would be akin to swallowing a serrated-edged knife. Perhaps something of a sidenote given the dangerously prickly nature of juvenile lancewood leaves, but they are also nutrient-poor, which may have provided an additional deterrent to would-be predators – as if that were needed.

Of course, once the lancewood attains a safe height beyond the reach of the moa, the need to expend extra energy in producing such specialised armature subsides, and the trees are able to repurpose energy for reproductive purposes.

Needless to say, such theories are somewhat circumstantial, given that moa are no longer around to provide opportunity to either prove or disprove them. However, studies on a similar *Pseudopanax* species, *P. chathamicus* (known in Māori as Hoho), from New Zealand's Chatham Islands tend to support these theories. Moas never made it to the Chatham Islands and the Chatham Island lancewood lacks both the changing leaf colours and the fearsome teeth associated with its more widespread relative. A coincidence? Unlikely, though that might be as close as we'll get to the answer.

COMMON HOLLY

Ilex aquifolium

Common holly is one of the most familiar evergreen trees in European woodlands, with a distribution that spans most of the continent, extending into northern Africa and parts of western Asia. It is also widely grown as an ornamental in gardens, with horticultural selections made for distinctive leaf or fruit characteristics too numerous to mention. However, its introduction to North America and popularity as a garden subject have seen it become invasive on the west coast and even Hawaii, and its planting is now actively discouraged. The small, red fruits (commonly known as berries, but technically drupes because of the hard shell that surrounds the seed) are toxic to humans but happily taken by birds, which disperse seeds to all corners, where they readily germinate and establish.

Although it is more than capable of attaining arborescent dimensions, common holly's principal use in garden settings is hedging, where it lends itself to being kept tidy and provides a year-round screen. It is also something of a ball-game deterrent – anyone who has had cause to retrieve a ball from a tightly trimmed holly hedge will know just how vicious the spiny leaves can be. Though not as easily worked as yew (*Taxus baccata*), its amenability to pruning is sufficient for it to be a popular subject for topiary, with trees being pruned into globes, cubes and all manner of whimsical animal shapes.

Glossy, thick and leathery, common holly leaves generally have wavy margins furnished with up to seven fine, sharp spines per side, although the number is wildly variable. Indeed, the leaves can appear hedgehog-like in their armature, or be entirely absent of spines.

Common holly leaves are spiny as an effective defence against browsing animals. In the wild, the trees are vulnerable to attack from a variety of ungulates, but over much of their range domesticated sheep and goats are the most common browsers. In the garden setting though, it is not browsing animals that are usually the problem, but the mechanical hedge trimmer that has become the prime 'predator'. Once attacked, a holly will respond by producing ever spinier leaves. Hence, it is the most often browsed and the tightest, most regularly sheared hedges that have the spiniest leaves.

Unlike trees such as lancewood (*Pseudopanax crassifolius*, see page 61), where the mechanism for producing heavily toothed leaves appears fixed up to a certain age or height, common holly responds immediately to threat by producing spiny leaves. By the same token, the tree is equally able to produce spineless leaves. In most cases, though, where browsing or pruning is not a threat, holly splits the difference and produces both, usually with more heavily spined leaves

low down and less spiny ones higher up. This makes evolutionary sense, given that it takes energy to produce extra
spines and that browsing is more likely to happen closer to
the ground.

The ability to quickly respond to frequent environmental
pressure by producing spiny leaves is a consequence of the
common holly modifying its DNA, although not its underlying
genetic code, in a process known as methylation. This process,
a kind of chemical triggering of action or modification of gene
expression (also known as epigenetic change), occurs in
humans too, when information is passed from one molecule
to another to protect or work to restore immune systems, for
example. In common holly, methylation causes genes to
repress spinescence and thus trigger the development of spineless leaves.

Beyond ornament and attracting bird life, common holly
has proved useful in a few less obvious ways. Planted next to
saplings of more readily browsed species, hollies have been
employed as 'nurse plants' to deter herbivory. And historically,
holly trees were felled so that their spineless upper leaves
could provide winter fodder for grazing animals.

Holly also has a long association with culture and religion.
In Christianity, the leaves and berries are strongly linked with
Christmas; the spiny leaves are said to recall Jesus' crown of
thorns, and the red berries his blood. In the British Isles,
ceremonial practices with holly go back at least to the pagan
Beltane festival (the equivalent of May Day), where its leaves
were burned alongside those of ivy. Common holly leaves
and branches were also used for wreaths and given as gifts
during the Roman midwinter festival of Saturnalia. Used for
decoration in homes and in wreaths, they were thought to be

protective because the spines stopped evil spirits from entering. To cut down a holly tree was, and still is by some, considered bad luck; the evergreen leaves are reputedly the source of mystical powers and represent eternal life.

The holly genus, *Ilex*, is amazingly diverse and widespread, with deciduous as well as evergreen trees and shrubs inhabiting both tropical and temperate zones worldwide. It is at its most diverse in parts of Southeast Asia and Malesia and in the tropical Americas, and contains more than 400 species. It is the only genus in the holly family, *Aquifoliaceae*, whose name (and epithet of common holly) comes from the Latin *aquifolius* meaning 'needle-leaved'; the name *Ilex* comes from the Latin for the European holm oak, *Quercus ilex* (see page 79), whose spine-margined juvenile leaves are similar to those of common holly.

Several *Ilex* species resemble common holly. The spiny American holly (*Ilex opaca*) would be a dead ringer were it not for its much duller leaves, while a number of East Asian hollies share similarly spiny leaves. All of them benefit from their leaves' protective effects, but not all *Ilex* bear spines, whether attacked by browsers or not. In fact, most species show little foliar resemblance to common holly at all, and the leaves of several have a use not commonly associated with the European species.

Yerba maté, a tea-like drink popular in Latin America, is made from the leaves of *Ilex paraguariensis*, a shrub or small tree native to parts of South America. Imported to the Levant in the nineteenth century and to South Africa in the early twentieth century, the leaves are now widely used as an ingredient in energy drinks, and are sold as tea and as a health food in Western supermarkets. Two North American holly species, *I. cassine* and *I. vomitoria*, were similarly used by Native Americans. Further south, *I. guayusa* is used as an ingredient in alcoholic drinks, as well as for an infusion and snuff used in ritualistic ceremonies and as a detoxifier. The caffeine-rich leaves of *Ilex* also contain theobromine, an alkaloid that was first characterised in chocolate (*Theobroma cacao*) and that has a similar effect on the human nervous system to caffeine. In China, the leaves of *Ilex kaushue* are used to make a bitter tea known as kuding, though sometimes another species entirely is used: *Ligustrum robustum* – a privet (in the olive family, Oleaceae). Coincidently, common privet (*Ligustrum vulgare*) is a familiar hedging plant in Europe, much like common holly, though neither sound as appealing a beverage choice as their exotic relatives.

SASSAFRAS

Sassafras albidum

Trees can make an impact with exceptional height, massive, spreading branches, flamboyant flowers or colourful fruit. Sassafras has none of those features, but still makes a singular, even unforgettable, impression.

A colony-forming deciduous tree native to forests and woodlands in the eastern United States, as far north as southern Ontario, sassafras flourishes best under the cold winter and hot and humid summer conditions that characterise the region. The species is common in abandoned fields and the trees are somewhat aggressive colonisers of disturbed places.

Nothing special? Well, just try to walk by without noticing the intense verdure of its unusual, tri-lobed, bi-lobed and unlobed leaves, or without smelling the sweet, old-time candy-shop aroma emanating from bruised or broken branches, exposed roots or the deeply furrowed, blocky bark.

Aromatic compounds are common in the laurel family, Lauraceae, to which sassafras belongs. They are mostly poisons and hence effective feeding deterrents. In most places, sassafras trees are unbothered by pests. The chemistry that provides this unexpectedly pleasant aroma is well studied, but may be surprising to some. The aromatic compound safrole is the major component of sassafras oil, which was once used in a variety of food products and cosmetics. In quantity, safrole is both carcinogenic and a liver poison in rats, and in humans it is known to induce abortions. Although it was once commonly used as an insect repellent, when applied directly to the skin sassafras oil can cause contact dermatitis in some individuals. Sassafras tea, traditionally prepared by steeping the bark of the roots in water, was once considered a refreshing pick-me-up and tonic and, before it was banned in the United States and elsewhere, sassafras oil was the primary flavouring in root beer.

Sassafras oil has the somewhat dubious distinction of being hallucinogenic when taken in large doses. This makes some sense when we know that safrole is a chemical precursor of the compounds that are used to make the recreational drugs MDMA (commonly known as ecstasy) and MDA. Originally harvested from *S. albidum* fruits and its root bark, safrole is found in all *Sassafras* species, as well the Brazilian *Ocotea odorifera* (also a member of the laurel family), which is commercially harvested for that compound. Safrole is also present to a lesser extent in anise (*Pimpinella anisum*), nutmeg (*Myristica fragrans*), cinnamon (*Cinnamomum* species) and black pepper (*Piper nigrum*).

Sassafras leaves could almost be described as unique, except that those of the other species – *S. randaiensis* from Taiwan and *S. tzumu* from China – share the shape-shifting trait. Foliar polymorphisms are not particularly rare in the plant world (as we have already seen), but they most often describe size differences between, for example the lusty, frequently exaggerated leaves on rapidly growing shoots and the smaller, more modest leaves on reproductively mature branches. Such examples might be found on any poplar (*Populus*) tree. Sassafras leaves are a different thing entirely. In their least elaborated form, the leaves are more or less elliptic in outline with a pointed to rounded tip. A number of leaves, usually the greater portion of them, will be endowed with a pair of lateral lobes that are similar in shape and size, but asymmetrical, at either side of a symmetrical central lobe. The gap between the lobes, known botanically as a sinus, is usually deep and narrow and, like the lobe margins, smooth-sided. Less common are bi-lobed leaves. On these, the single lateral lobe is more like an afterthought, an appendage not yet fully formed. This is the derivation of the alternate common name 'mitten plant', and if one looks carefully, both left- and right-handed mittens can usually be found on any tree. There are even, occasionally, five-lobed leaves. But why any lobes at all?

There is a huge range of leaf lobe patterns in the plant world. Maples (*Acer* species) and oaks (*Quercus* species) are probably the two most familiar examples. While maples frequently have radiating, or 'palmate', lobes, oaks mostly exhibit lateral, or 'pinnate' lobing. Sassafras lobes, when present, are of the palmate type, and it is readily apparent when viewing the leaf how the main veins radiate from a point above where the petiole and leaf blade meet. Lobing is generally interpreted as an adaptation to reduce overheating in leaves. Like the fins on a radiator, leaf lobes help the leaf to dissipate heat. This is why the leaves on the shady side of an oak tree are often larger with less well-defined lobes than those on the sunny side of a tree. Still, the variability in the amount of lobing (from none to three or five) in the sassafras leaf suggests that there might be something else going on here. The most compelling explanation, which is borne out by the relative positions of the different kinds of leaves on the branches, is as follows.

The first-produced leaves of the season are small and unlobed, but as the season progresses daytime temperatures become increasingly hot and, as the stems elongate, the newer leaves bear lobes. Lobed leaves are a benefit as they stay cool while photosynthesising. At the same time, they do not over-shade the earliest leaves. If growth continues into the late summer, the leaves once again become unlobed, since the angle of the sun and the air temperature at this time of year are unlikely to burn an unlobed leaf. Corroborating this theory is the fact that shaded sassafras trees and those grown in cooler climates tend not to have lobed leaves at all. A well grown sassafras – that is, one situated in a hot and sunny site – will usually produce spectacularly coloured, mostly orange to vermillion-red leaves in autumn.

So, there are plenty of reasons to celebrate the sassafras tree. Traditional root beer flavoured with sassafras oil was significantly more flavourful than commercial root beer flavoured with safrole-free sassafras extract, or no sassafras at all – and the oil is still manufactured in some places, though not legally. Leaving aside the more questionable aspects and nefarious merits of its biochemistry, however, there are still a couple of other valuable uses. When burned, the aromatic compounds in sassafras wood produce a rainbow of flame colours – mostly blues, oranges and yellows – and the combusting wood has a wonderful fragrance. While sassafras firewood is seldom recommended by the wood stove crowd because it burns quickly and at a low temperature (too few BTUs), it was the most popular fireplace fuel in early Hollywood colour movies because of its beautiful colours.

Perhaps the most common use for sassafras is for filé (fee-lay) powder, an important ingredient in Louisiana Creole cuisine. Filé is a spicy herb and thickening agent made from the ground and powdered leaves of *S. albidum*, probably most famously used in the dish filé gumbo, a thick soup or stew. Sassafras leaves have a negligible amount of safrole, so are considered safe to use. The Choctaw Indians of the southern United States introduced filé powder to Acadian settlers – Cajuns, in the local parlance – French-speaking people who had fled the Canadian Maritime provinces during the French and British hostilities in the mid-eighteenth century. The rest as they say, is history.

HOLM OAK

Quercus ilex

Considering that there are 500 or so species of oak (*Quercus*) that occur across the world, and the great diversity in crown size and form that they display, it's no wonder that there is also huge variation in the size of their leaves. Some of the largest leaves occur in the Japanese daimyo oak (*Quercus dentata*, see page 123) – they can sometimes be over a foot long – while the smallest are attributed to the aptly named *Quercus microphylla* (*micro* = small, *phylla* = leaf), a tiny shrub from Mexico.

As diverse as they are in leaf size, oaks also display considerable variation in how long they hold on to their leaves. While the European English oak (*Quercus robur*) is fully deciduous, environmental pressures impacting leaves begin to change as habitats vary to the south and east around the Mediterranean region, and the strategies to combat them get a little more specialised. The Algerian oak (*Q. canariensis*), a native of northern Africa and the Iberian Peninsula (and not the Canary Islands, as the specific epithet suggests), is semi-evergreen, dropping its old leaves as soon as its new leaves emerge, while cork oak (*Quercus suber*), from the western Mediterranean, is a 'leaf exchanger', with old leaves swapped for new ones within the year. Holm oak, widespread and common throughout the Mediterranean Basin, is considered a true evergreen, with leaves that persist for between one and three years.

Though the archetypal oak leaf has rounded lobes much like those of the English or daimyo oak (in oversized form), there is a wonderful diversity of forms among oak leaves. Several appear to mimic species in other genera and, usefully, some of these have been named accordingly. There is maple-leaved oak (*Quercus acerifolia*; *Acer* = maple) from Arkansas, in the United States, while chestnut-leaved oak (*Quercus castaneifolia; Castanea* = chestnut) comes from the Caucasus. Myrtle oak (*Quercus myrtifolia*) is so named for a foliar resemblance to myrtle (*Myrtus communis*), although this visual association is somewhat more tenuous.

It is perhaps not surprising that the specific epithet of the holm oak, *ilex*, also gives an indication of its appearance. *Ilex* is the classical Latin name for this tree, the generic name given to the hollies, while holm (from Middle English *holin*) means 'prickly'. And at first sight, it would be forgivable to confuse a holm oak leaf with that of a common holly (*Ilex aquifolium*). Indeed, holly oak is another common name. Heterophyllous, like holly, in youth holm oak leaves are sparsely (or occasionally densely) spined with sharp teeth, before transitioning on reproductive shoots to a longer, narrow shape with finer, less prominent marginal teeth. While the leaves of both species are variable, the trick, as with the identification of many trees, is to turn a leaf over. A holly leaf has a shiny, hairless lower surface, whereas that of holm oak is finely white-felted.

The resemblance to holly is not so unusual in oaks as, like common holly, their spinescence is an adaptation for deterring herbivory. Oaks being common in arid lands where browsers are common, spinescent leaves are an effective protection. Another species, *Quercus aquifolioides*, is also named for its foliar similarity to holly, but in this case the author of this epithet doubled down, leaving no doubt as to what these leaves resembled (*aquifolioides* means 'like *Ilex aquifolium*'). Native to high-elevation habitats in south-central China and Tibet, this too can be distinguished from holm oak by turning a leaf over; its undersides are yellow-felted.

In the wild, holm oak is a dominant component of sclero-phyllous woodland. This is a habitat characterised by trees and shrubs that have tough, leathery, evergreen foliage adapted to limiting water loss. This vegetation type is typical of the world's Mediterranean-type climates, where summers are hot and dry, sometimes even with no rain at all, and the winters mild and wet. As well as the Mediterranean Basin itself, these climates occur in parts of California in the United States and Baja California in Mexico; central Chile; the Cape Region of South Africa; and south-western and south Australia. Despite an extreme lack of water during a good part of the year, these areas harbour impressive floristic diver-sity, including hundreds of sclerophyllous species in several different plant families. Aside from the Mediterranean Basin, oaks occur in California and Baja California, where their growth forms are as diverse as they are anywhere. Sclerophylly in these geographically distant areas is another example of convergent evolution, where common adaptive traits evolve independently in comparable environments. The word sclerophyllous relates to sclerenchyma, itself derived from the Greek *skleros*, meaning hard, and *enchyma*, translating as 'infused with'. Sclerenchyma cells contain lignin – the same compound as in wood – which provides structural support to cells and the tissues they comprise. These cells are particularly abundant in the leaves of holm oak, helping to provide their characteristic toughness.

Coping with a scarce water is a serious problem. A common strategy is slow, compact growth and small, tough leaves that are oriented parallel to the sun's rays. Many oaks, including holm oak, adopt this strategy when conditions demand it. In tandem with getting by with less, many plants have the ability to slow down water loss from their leaves, though some species are better at this than others. European alder (*Alnus glutinosa*) is not very good at regulating water loss. As a riparian species, growing along watercourses, it doesn't need to be particularly water-thrifty. The situation for holm oak is markedly different, however, as it grows on dry soils and has to endure the heat of the Mediterranean sun, meaning that limiting water loss is a must – which is where the hairs come in. A fine pelt of hairs helps create an insulative boundary layer on the leaf's surface. In holm oak, this layer is thick, helping to reflect light but also keeping the leaf cool and reducing the amount of water that escapes to the atmosphere. Holm oak leaves tend to be hairier under consistently droughty conditions than where moisture is more freely available.

Being evergreen and subject to cold winter temperatures, a holm oak needs an adaptive strategy that can protect its leaves during the coldest parts of the year. To accomplish this the leaf margins typically curl under, thus reducing the amount of surface exposed to the elements. But the tree also possesses an impressive ability to direct internal compounds to where they are most required, which can help preserve the integrity and functionality of the photosynthetic apparatus. Exposed, sun-adapted leaves manufacture sunscreen-like antioxidants, for example. As well, starches, lipids and sugars are pumped into the leaves for the winter to create antifreeze, which helps prevent intercellular water from freezing and rupturing leaf cells.

Like oriental plane (*Platanus orientalis*, see page 307), holm oak has long since been valued as a shade tree, similarly being used to shield Greek scholars of old from the summer sun as they studied. The Romans additionally valued holm oak leaves for use as sheep bedding, although, as the leaves become hard as they dry, they probably wouldn't have been the sheep's first choice.

The species lends itself to hedging and topiary pruning, and examples of large, carefully shaped trees are a feature of Italian and 'Italian-style' gardens. Holm oak has also gained use as a landscape tree in parkland settings, though its invasive tendencies in parts of southern Britain have seen it being actively discouraged in some quarters. Its success in climates with cold winters – at least colder than where it is native – is testament to the tree's versatility, thanks in no small part to the adaptability of its leaves – features that will likely become even more valuable in a future with a less predictable climate.

PRACTICAL PLANTS

We use a tree to furrow the seas and to bring the
lands nearer together, we use a tree for building
houses; even the images of the deities were
made from trees.

PLINY THE ELDER

The list of plants that humankind have found uses for is a stag-geringly large inventory. Even for leaves alone this is a humbling catalogue. People will utilise as much of a plant as is ultimately practical – and with trees the broad utility of wood definitely comes to mind, but leaves often have very specific uses. Some are widely recognised – raffia, for example, is familiar to both gardeners and crafters – while others are not well known outside of their native regions. The massive leaves of the majestic Bismarck palm present themselves to Madagascans wholly intact from the tree, ready for any local roofing project. Another Madagascar native, the traveller's palm, also provides ready-made construc-tion materials from its leaves. Those of thatch screw-pine must first be softened and sewn, and they are used for both sails and the side walls of houses in the South Pacific islands. A highly notable timber species, teak also gives us leaves essential for a couple of valuable cultures – one entomological and the other fungal. On the other hand, some leaves, like those of the ornamental daimyo oak, are prized for their size and beauty in culinary display in Japan. Finally, white mulberry leaves and silkworms tell us much about the creativity and innovative instincts of people who lived 6,500 years ago.

BISMARCK PALM

Bismarckia nobilis

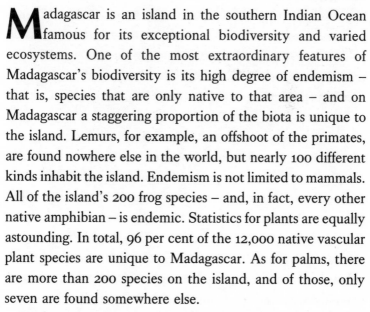

Madagascar is an island in the southern Indian Ocean famous for its exceptional biodiversity and varied ecosystems. One of the most extraordinary features of Madagascar's biodiversity is its high degree of endemism – that is, species that are only native to that area – and on Madagascar a staggering proportion of the biota is unique to the island. Lemurs, for example, an offshoot of the primates, are found nowhere else in the world, but nearly 100 different kinds inhabit the island. Endemism is not limited to mammals. All of the island's 200 frog species – and, in fact, every other native amphibian – is endemic. Statistics for plants are equally astounding. In total, 96 per cent of the 12,000 native vascular plant species are unique to Madagascar. As for palms, there are more than 200 species on the island, and of those, only seven are found somewhere else.

With such great diversity, one would think that no one

palm could stand out from all the rest, but Bismarck palm does that in spades. The majority of Madagascar's palm diversity is represented in tropical rainforests in the country's north-east, but Bismarck palm is native to the more arid western side, where it resides predominantly in savannah grasslands and sometimes grows in extensive, forest-like stands. The palm itself is a giant, with a massively thick, solitary trunk, producing equally impressive, green or sometimes steely-blue, fan-shaped leaves that form a symmetrical, spheroid crown. The petioles of these mammoth leaves are spirally arranged around the trunk and sparsely covered in contrasting shaggy brown hairs. The attachment of the petioles to the trunk is a beautiful example of structural engineering. Each leaf overlaps several beneath. As the palm grows upward, adding more leaves, the petioles diverge either left or right, alternating such that the weight of any one leaf is supported at its base by a strong weave of outer petioles. Though this architecture is not unique to Bismarck palm, the size of the petiole bases around the stout trunk makes the pattern especially appealing. The blue-leaved variant of the species is particularly sought after in ornamental horticulture.

Bismarck palm is so large and handsome that it is widely considered one of the most ornamental of all palms – the specific epithet *nobilis* means 'grand'. In a rare instance of naming a plant for a political figure, German botanical explorers named the palm in 1881 for the German Chancellor, Otto von Bismarck (1815–1898). This was soon after the Franco–Prussian war, a victory for Bismarck and a humiliating loss for Napoleon III. Not surprisingly, this riled the French colonial masters in Madagascar and their botanical counterparts in Paris, who tried, unsuccessfully, to change the palm's scientific name.

The palm family, Arecaceae, represents a surprising diversity of plant forms, including trees, climbers, shrubs and even stemless plants. Palms can grow as solitary stems or in clusters, but common to them all is the single meristem, the region of actively dividing cells located in the crown at the apex of the trunk. A peculiarity of the palms is that if this growing point is damaged or removed, the stem almost invariably dies. Anyone who has handled palms can attest that their leaves and stems are fibrous and tough, but meristematic tissues are another matter altogether. These tissues may be hidden in the crown, but they are soft and vulnerable to predation or injury. For this reason, spines and prickles are protective adaptations and common features in many palms where herbivores have a taste for them, and spiny palms are exceedingly common on the African mainland, where elephants or giraffes and other ungulates are also frequent. Four hundred kilometres away in Madagascar, where there are no such megafaunal herbivores, there is only a single native palm that bears spines.

Most people would recognise only two types of palms. Pinnate-leaved palms bear leaves in which the slender more-or-less uniform leaflets are supported on an arching central axis. Coconut (*Cocos nucifera*), date (*Phoenix dactylifera*) and the ubiquitous indoor areca palm (*Dypsis lutescens*) all follow this pattern. Palmate-leaved palms, like the cold-hardy Chusan palm (*Trachycarpus fortunei*), European fan palm (*Chamaerops humilis*) or indeed the Bismarck palm, have leaves with a stout petiole that terminates in a broad, pleated, fan-like photosynthetic surface or blade. In the Bismarck palm, the blade can be up to 3 metres across, and the sturdy petiole can exceed 2.5 metres in length. The massive, fibrous leaves are handy for a variety of uses, including basketry, where the blade is split, and notably for construction and roofing, when it is left intact. Conveniently, the weight of the leaves is sufficient for the petiole to break off cleanly from the trunk when the older leaves are eventually shed. This leaves the tree with a smooth trunk and makes the task of collecting the leaves all the more straightforward.

Despite the fact that the Bismarck palm is common in Madagascar and enormously popular as an ornamental, little is known about its natural pollinators or the animals that aid in the dispersal of its plum-sized fruits. And it's likely that we'll never know for sure, as many of Madagascar's established plant–animal interactions have been thoroughly disrupted. Sadly, more than 80 per cent of Madagascar's original forests have been lost, and the already sobering numbers of plants and animals that are listed as Extinct, Critically Endangered, Endangered or Vulnerable continues to grow. Estimates are that more than 80 per cent of the island's endemic palms are on the brink of extinction. Even still, the tiny amount of remaining protected forest land reminds us of the magnificent biodiversity that once flourished across Madagascar.

PALMIER RAFFIA

Raphia farinifera

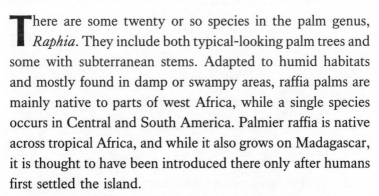

There are some twenty or so species in the palm genus, *Raphia*. They include both typical-looking palm trees and some with subterranean stems. Adapted to humid habitats and mostly found in damp or swampy areas, raffia palms are mainly native to parts of west Africa, while a single species occurs in Central and South America. Palmier raffia is native across tropical Africa, and while it also grows on Madagascar, it is thought to have been introduced there only after humans first settled the island.

Palmier raffia has a relatively stout, solitary stem that can grow to an imposing 9 metres in height. While this can be impressive, it is the leaves that are extraordinary. They have been measured at an incredible 21 metres long (about the length of a cricket wicket), with up to 150 leaflets on each side of the rachis. The petiole can be an equally remarkable 6 metres long, and the individual leaflets each more than

2 metres long. Specimens have around a dozen leaves borne at the tip of the stem, the leaves arching up and outward from the erect orange petioles, radiating like green ostrich feathers. But as if 21-metre leaves weren't long enough, those of another raffia palm, *R. regalis* (which translates as 'royal' or 'regal raffia'), are bigger, measuring up to 25 metres from the base of the petiole to the tip of the rachis, which makes them the longest leaves in the plant kingdom. Though remarkable, the super-sized leaves are somewhat tricky to collect and store for comparative study, to say nothing of the trials of navigating swampy ground to actually locate the palms in the first place. There are, therefore, still plenty of questions around *Raphia* classification, though work to establish relationships within the genus continues.

Consistent with the astonishing dimensions of the leaves, palmier raffia's inflorescence can be up to 3 metres across. The tree is capable of producing flowers only after around 20 years. After fruiting, which takes between three and six years to complete, the tree dies. This monocarpic (*mono* = one, *carpo* = fruit) life strategy occurs in all species of *Raphia* as well as a few other palms, although it is otherwise rare among trees.

Given the immense size of their foliar parts, it is not surprising that raffia palms would have many uses. Some 100 different examples have been recorded, although not all are used for their leaves. Perhaps more extraordinary still, there is one *Raphia* species, *R. gabonica*, with no recorded uses at all. Palmier raffia is one of the most thoroughly utilised species, though several others are used for similar purposes, depending on their local availability.

Among the most significant uses of leaves is for its fibres, which, while the leaves are young, are stripped from the developing leaflets and, once dried, are twisted to form threads that are then used to weave mats, baskets, hats and toys, among other products. Of great cultural importance in parts of Central Africa, clothes woven from raffia fibres are worn in traditional ceremonies. In pre-colonial times, raffia cloth was used as currency and bartered for goods. The fibres are also a source of horticultural twine used for tying and supporting garden plants, and especially in floristry for tying bouquets. Raffia twine's popularity with Western gardeners is mostly due to it being a natural fibre that is soft, flexible and strong, and ultimately biodegradable.

As the leaves age, their practical utility changes, but their value does not. The toughened, leaflet midribs are used to make brooms, while older leaflets, woven together, are used for thatching roofs. Raffia thatch lasts around five years and keeps buildings cooler than synthetic alternatives, while also dampening the sound of heavy rainfall; thus it is more conducive than synthetic materials to a good night's sleep.

The leaves' huge, strong petioles and rachises are also used variously and are referred to as 'bamboo' owing to their visual likeness and similar utility to those distantly related plants. These are used for fences and walls as well as in roofing, as support for the leaflet thatch. They are also used in basket weaving and as floats for fishing nets.

Raffia's uses are not always strictly practical, either. Across parts of central Africa, raffia palm leaves are used to make a variety of musical instruments. These include the traditional harp-zither, the *mvet*. Ingeniously, a 1- to 2-metre length of leaf rachis holds three or four strings, which are, as well, made from parts of the rachis, peeled away in narrow strips from its edges. These are stretched over a central, wooden bridge and played from either side. The raffia strings do not last for long, however, and so metal ones are preferred where possible. Pieces of the petiole are also used to amplify the instrument's sound and are used similarly to make soundboards for the *támìntúbà*, a one-stringed harp of the Bagyeli in Cameroon.

Raffia rachises are also used to make a lamellaphone, or thumb piano, known as a *sanza* in central Africa and a *mbira* in east Africa, where small, tongue-like lamellae are mounted on a soundboard and played with the fingers and thumbs. The lamellae can be made from the outermost layers of the rachis, while the soundboard is made by joining three or four petioles together.

But of course, it is not just the leaves of raffia palm that are utilised, and other parts of the plant also have many uses. Trees are tapped for their sap to make wine, which is drunk ceremonially at both royal enthronements and family celebrations. Sharing wine to show gratitude at both business and social occasions is considered an important act in rural villages in Cameroon. Tapping trees for sap is a dangerous occupation, though, and accidents and injury are all too common, while the product itself is quick to spoil.

In some species, raffia palm fruits are edible, and are consumed raw or cooked. Their shells are used for buttons, and seeds for decoration. Of course it must also be noted that raffia palms, and particularly palmier raffia, make impressive ornamentals, at least for those who have the climate and the space to grow them.

Raffia palms are then the very definition of a multipurpose plant – except for the rare *R. gabonica*. Still, it was first described only in 2015, so there is still time for it to reveal its uses – if, that is, it has time: *R. gabonica* is already thought to be threatened with extinction. A lack of utility might turn out to be a blessing.

TEAK

Tectona grandis

Teak is widely recognised as one of the most valuable of tropical hardwoods. It is the favoured timber for boat-building and the manufacture of outdoor furniture, and is widely used in the production of veneer. Teak is also one of the most prolific cultivated timber crops in the world. Many of us are familiar with the rich-brown, fine-grained, oily wood but, as with other hardwoods, consumers are largely unaware of the origins of the tropical commodities that they might sail in, eat their supper on or cover their cabinet fronts and floors with. Nor would they recognise what any of these trees actually looks like. And who could fault them?

As trees go, *Tectona grandis* has a statuesque form, with an attractively fluted and buttressed base, and an open scaffold of spreading branches that can reach upwards of 30 metres. The lush canopy of softly hairy leaves is seasonally adorned on mature individuals with a halo of tiny, white flowers. As an open-grown specimen, teak is a handsome giant of a tree with a high, rounded crown.

Although teak is a member of the mint family, Lamiaceae, it bears little resemblance to its more familiar, square-stemmed relatives such as sage or spearmint. Until recently, in fact, *Tectona* was placed in a different family altogether, the verbena family, Verbenaceae. Nevertheless, there are a few features that make a connection with the mints more comprehensible. Even a cursory look at a typical mint reveals its distinctive leaf arrangement; each of the paired leaves along the stems is arranged at right angles to the pair above, and the pair below. Looking down from the tip of a stem, the leaves form four perfect ranks. The same four-ranked, 'decussate' arrangement is apparent in teak, although the leaves can also adopt a whorled arrangement, and are considerably larger and less aromatic than most other mints.

While it might seem obvious that leaves are fundamental to plant growth, their size, spacing and number in the canopy have a lot to do with a plant's productivity. Large leaves make a sizeable photosynthetic platform, and teak leaves are very large indeed. It has been postulated that the heat accumulated in a large leaf can drive photosynthesis at a higher rate. Assuming that light, water and carbon dioxide are not in short supply, a greater leaf area means more wood, as the wood in trees is primarily made up of carbon, which is taken up in photosynthesis. Of course, in the tropical sun, big leaves can heat up to the point that their internal chemistry is denatured and normal metabolic processes crippled. Countering this are two phenomena. The first is the boundary-layer effect provided by hairs that clothe the leaves. Like in holm oak, dense hairs create an insulating blanket of air next to the surface, and this helps to moderate temperatures inside the leaf. More important is the role of evapotranspiration, which is the loss of water vapour through stomata (pores for gas exchange). Up to a point, the more water that is lost through the stomata, the cooler the leaves. Although the cooling effect is called 'the latent heat of evaporation', the science behind the effect is neither difficult nor unfamiliar. As the water within the leaf evaporates as it exits the stomata, it must absorb heat to make the change from liquid water to water vapour. That heat is carried away with the vapour into the atmosphere. Perspiration has the same effect on our skin.

Teak is native to parts of South and Southeast Asia where the climate is hot and humid, as well as rainy for most, if not all, of the year. In areas with seasonally dry periods, teak trees lose their leaves until the rains return. This makes ecological sense, as without an adequate supply of moisture for evapotranspiration, the leaves would easily overheat and dry up.

The species grows naturally in hilly terrain in dense forests, areas mostly inaccessible to all but the most adventurous or determined travellers or, sadly, to timber poachers. In terms of world production, plantation teak now outnumbers naturally grown teak by a wide margin. Tourists are unlikely to encounter teak plantations, despite the fact that they exist nearly everywhere across the tropical and subtropical world. In most cases, plantations have replaced huge swathes of previously inaccessible, species-rich forest, and are located well away from beaches and nature reserves.

Teak plantations are invariably bleak, monoculture stands, consisting of row upon row of uniform-aged trees. In a crowded plantation, lower branches and leaves are quickly shed. On the ground below, only dried-up leaves, twigs and scattered fragments of the soft grey bark are usually visible. To say that teak loses much of its majesty when planted this way is a considerable understatement. Both the leaves and bark are known to be allelopathic – that is, they produce compounds that can reduce the establishment and growth of other plants – and these natural herbicides, as well as the overwhelming shade from above, help to keep the ground free of competing vegetation. But because in teak plantations the ground is bare, the soil is exposed to the erosive effects of the heavy rains that are characteristic of these regions, which has wider implications than just the loss of soil and a grim-looking view.

Although they are normally pest-resistant trees because of the oils in their wood, the uniformity and lack of biodiversity in a teak plantation creates conditions that promote the proliferation of pests, such as the teak defoliator (*Hyblaea puera*). The defoliator is the larva (caterpillar) of an innocuous-looking native moth that was previously of minor importance, but now regularly ravages teak plantations. The caterpillars feed on the leaves, often completely defoliating entire trees, leaving only tattered remnants of green around the leaves' skeletal midribs hanging from the branches. The caterpillars then pupate and drop to the ground. In parts of rural Indonesia where teak has been established in plantations (it is not native there), these cocoons are collected and the pupae eaten by local villagers. In biodiverse forests, outbreaks of the pest are only occasional and the trees easily recover. Though they reduce opportunities for humans to benefit from an additional protein source, the numerous other predators that are found in intact forests – including various birds and primates – help keep the teak defoliator in check, thus relieving pressure on the trees.

Teak wood is highly resistant to rotting and because of that local people have traditionally used it in construction and especially for bridge-building and other projects where wood comes into regular contact with water. Teak leaves also figure highly in traditional uses across tropical Asia. In folk medicine, the leaves are recommended in treatments for (among other ailments) dysentery, anaemia, weakness, malaria, sore throat and tuberculosis. Teak seed oil has even been identified as a hair-growth promoter – strange that big pharma hasn't leapt on that one. In parts of southern India, the leaves are used in making a dumpling known as *pellakai gatti*, where prepared jackfruit (*Artocarpus heterophyllus*) batter is poured into teak leaves and steamed. In Java, teak leaves are added to water in which jackfruit is boiled to add a dark brown colour to the dish known as *gudeg*. Perhaps the most unusual use for teak leaves is as a tempeh starter, a practice that also originates in Java. Tempeh is a fermented tofu-like product, increasingly popular with people who espouse a vegan diet. It is usually made with soybeans and has a white crust that resembles the rind of some soft cheeses. The fungus required for the fermentation (*Rhizopus oligosporus*) is found naturally on the downy leaf-backs of teak and coastal hibiscus (*Hibiscus tiliaceus*), and both are used in the local Javanese manufacture of tempeh.

THATCH SCREW-PINE

Pandanus tectorius

The screw-pines are a group of tropical shrubs and trees with semi-woody stems and evergreen, strap-like leaves. They are unusual plants and very distinctive. Most species form low trees with hefty, leaning stems marked with prominent, undulating, more-or-less horizontal leaf scars, and supported by long, tube-like prop-roots that allow plants to grow in shifting sands. *Pandanus* stems are often marked by both aerial roots and spines derived from aborted aerial roots, and the leaves, which are crowded toward the branch tips, are spirally arranged and, in most cases, oriented into three separate ranks. The leaves are typically adorned with spiny midribs and margins, but spineless forms are known and often purposely cultivated. The fruit heads of pandanus are extraordinary. There are derived from a pineapple-like head of female flowers (the male flowers are borne in drooping clusters on separate plants). Once fertilised, the whole develops into a heavy, roughly globose structure made up of multiple, close-fitting, seed-containing structures known as phalanges or keys that are attached to a central core. In some species the heads are round, but in others more elongated. The phalanges are buoyant and sufficiently waterproof to protect the seeds within while floating, sometimes for months, in the ocean. Like the coconut, ocean currents are the primary method of distribution for the thatch screw-pine. The family, Pandanaceae, is related to the yuccas and the palms, sharing with those plants a spiral leaf arrangement and leaves with sheathing bases. Otherwise, the screw-pines look like nothing else.

Screw-pines are not pines. In fact, *Pandanus* are monocots, flowering plants that produce, in most of their members, parallel-veined leaves, flower parts in threes and a vasculature characterised by water-conducting cells that are produced in bundles, like groups of straws, scattered through the fibrous stems. Monocots – short for monocotyledonous plants – are so named because their germinated seedlings start out with a single seed leaf (*mono* = one + *cotyledon* = seed leaf). The vast majority of monocots are herbaceous plants, like orchids, gingers and grasses (bamboos are grasses, but that's another matter entirely). True pines, which are conifers, as well as dicotyledonous plants – flowering plants that have two seed leaves – are the only plants that have a vascular cambium. This is a cylinder of dividing cells immediately to the inside of the stem. New cells are produced to the outside of the vascular cylinder, and this allows the plant to expand in girth. As a tree grows, the cells to the inside of the cambium die and become lignified, forming wood, while those to the outside of the dividing cells also die and typically become corky, forming bark. In dicot stems and roots, only the cells between these two tissue systems are living. In monocots, because the vascular bundles are scattered through the stem tissues, they don't have the same capacity to expand in girth or produce true wood; for these reasons, monocots are more limited in size, durability and strength. Despite those limitations, some monocots can become impressively large, and the thatch screw-pine can form a well-branched tree to about 15 metres tall. Still, the trunk and branches are only ever a maximum diameter of about 25 centimetres.

Native to the Pacific Islands, parts of Southeast Asia and northern Australia, thatch screw-pine is usually found growing in areas close to, or directly on, ocean beaches at the strand-line (high water mark). The species is much at home in these environments, as it is tolerant of drought, flooding, strong winds, saline soils and salt-spray. Its leaves are variable in size and shape, up to 3 metres long and 16 centimetres wide. The leaves are V-shaped in cross-section, particularly toward the base, and are able to channel rainwater to the stems and branches, whereupon the water then runs down the stems and prop roots to soak into the ground directly around the roots. This is a useful adaptation, as moisture is often drained away very quickly in a sandy environment. Stiff and ascending when young, the mature leaves bend strongly down toward the tips, hanging in casual, swaying curtains of foliage. The persistent skirt of older dead leaves provides shelter and nesting opportunities to a variety of small animals.

People have been making selections of thatch screw-pine across the entire range of the species for the various charac-teristics of the fruits, branches and leaves for as long as they have inhabited the places where it grows. Selections are normally specific to a place and use, or set of uses, and each typically has a name in the local language. While thatch screw-pine can be easily grown from seed, selected forms must be propagated vegetatively; that is, by rooting detached pieces of the stem. In this way every successive individual of the selected plant is genetically the same. This makes them technically cultivars (a portmanteau word derived from culti-vated + variety).

Because the leaves of thatch screw-pine are stiff and leathery, and often fiercely spine-margined, some processing is usually involved before they can be effectively manipulated. Even spineless leaves must first be softened by soaking in the ocean or boiling. Thatch screw-pine leaves are used exten-sively, not least as material for thatching traditional houses (*tectorius* means 'of rooftops'), but also for all kinds of weaving for baskets, mats and screens and, even, formerly, for canoe sails. While the poles and branches are used in construction, the prop roots are sometimes employed to make basket handles, paintbrushes or skipping ropes, or processed to make dyes and traditional medicines. A number of *Pandanus* species have leaves that are used in cooking – the fragrant pandan, also widely known as pandan leaf (*Pandanus amaryllifolius*), originally native to the Moluccas, is widely employed in South and Southeast Asian cuisine, for example – but the leaves of thatch screw-pine are neither fragrant nor edible.

Along with their pollinising duties, male flowers are valued for their fragrance. They are used to scent coconut oil and tapa cloth and to make garlands. As in other *Pandanus* species, the fruit heads of thatch screw-pine are enormously variable. They are generally globose, consisting of up to 200 wedge-shaped keys. In some selections the heads are small and in others they can be the size of a basketball, and the keys particularly fleshy and as large as ice cream bars. When ripe, the whole head becomes bright orange-red, attracting sulphur-crested cockatoos. For people, palatability is a criterion upon which the fruits are judged. Some selections are eaten fresh, while others are deemed better once preserved, and still others used as bait for catching lobsters. But actual edibility is another important measure, and particularly fibrous keys may be dried and used for fuel, paintbrushes, or as floats for fishing nets. The seeds within the keys are sometimes roasted or eaten raw, and some cultivars produce seeds that apparently taste of coconut.

Like so many plants that are used by traditional societies, the diversity of cultivated thatch screw-pines is diminishing. People across the species' range have become more urbanised and less interested in traditional methods and, along with the loss of culture, the destruction of habitat by fire, deforestation and development are all taking a toll on the range of cultivars available.

TRAVELLER'S PALM

Ravenala madagascariensis

Few trees have a structure so unlikely that they deserve the 'you couldn't make that up' comment, but the traveller's palm is definitely one of them. One expects the extraordinary in plants (and animals) that are only found in Madagascar, but traveller's palm is exceptional even for a Madagascan endemic. *Ravenala* is not even a palm, but a genus in the bird-of-paradise-flower family, Strelitziaceae, closely related to *Strelitzia*, which is commonly seen as a cut flower in florist shops specialising in the flamboyant. In both *Strelitzia* and *Ravenala*, the leaves are produced in two distinctively flattened ranks. The unfurling leaves push older ones to either side, resulting in an attractive fan. Other plants are known for this kind of arrangement – Iris is a familiar example – but it's not a particularly common pattern in the plant world.

The leaves of the traveller's palm can be enormous. They arise from a stout, solitary or occasionally basally branched stem that can be up to 20 metres tall. From here, 20 to 35 leaves extend to nearly 10 metres in length. Each leaf has an extensive clasping base and an equally long, cylindrical petiole that supports a huge, banana-leaf-like blade. The leaf bases, which are yellowish, tightly overlap such that they create a giant, semicircular base from which the petioles splay out like an exotic headdress. As if this were not remarkable enough, in every individual tree the leaf fan is only ever oriented east and west. This reliable compass orientation can be very helpful in the tropics where the sun is mostly high overhead in the daytime, and is the likely reason for the name traveller's palm. There is another, often cited but less plausible, reason for the name, which is that thirsty travellers can take advantage of the sizeable rain-filled petiole bases; but the liquid in these stagnant reservoirs is more likely to give travellers something else entirely. The crown shape of the traveller's palm is so recognisable as belonging to Madagascar's exotic and threatened flora that it has been adopted by the plant conservation charity Botanic Gardens Conservation International (BGCI) for its logo.

Being so large, the leaves are commonly used in construction – especially house building – but all parts of the traveller's palm are used by local Madagascans. The fleshy heart of the tree is sometimes cooked as a vegetable, and is used in folk and veterinary medicine as well. The petioles are used in wall and roof construction and the petiole fibres used to make rope. The trunks, which can be as large as 60 centimetres in diameter, are traditionally planked for flooring.

Ravenala species are monocots; that is, plants with fleshy

or fibrous, but not woody, stems. Most monocots have small flowers with parts in threes. Those adapted to open environments frequently have capsular, or at least dry fruits, and narrow leaves with parallel veins. Grasses are the obvious example. The majority of shade-adapted monocots, in contrast, have evolved broader leaves with secondarily branched venation and fleshy, animal-dispersed fruits. But the traveller's palm does not exactly fit the mould. Although it is widely distributed in open country across eastern Madagascar, its broad leaves are more typical of trees adapted to a protected, forested setting, and its fruits, while dry – as would be expected – have seeds that are endowed with fleshy arils; an oil-rich seed appendage that attracts animals.

The traveller's palm leaf has pinnate-parallel veins. This describes a vein architecture where the ultimate veins arise more or less perpendicular to a main, axial vein. While broad leaves are efficient light-intercepting organs, they can suffer considerable wind damage in the open. Like an exposed banana leaf, the traveller's palm leaf tears conveniently along the parallel veins, thus reducing drag in the wind. And while the leaves can look tattered and even feathery, they are generally no worse for the tearing, and the photosynthetic surface area is barely diminished. In fact, the tearing is probably advantageous to plants in the open, as the smaller leaf surface area and flapping action are both effective in reducing heat loading, while an increase in edge area tends to promote radiative heat loss.

The centre of the fan of leaves is where the flowers are produced and, in the traveller's palm, the flower stalks are fittingly impressive. They extend upwards well into the crown and bear multiple boat-shaped bracts in twisted stacks. Each bract partially encloses an inflorescence of showy, white, nectar-filled flowers. This is much like the arrangement in the southern African genus *Strelitzia*, except that bird-of-paradise flowers are brightly coloured and usually held well above the crown of foliage to better attract avian pollinators. There are, of course, birds in Madagascar, but the pollination duties of the traveller's palm have been taken on by the black-and-white ruffed lemur (*Varecia variegata*). These long-tailed, cat-sized arboreal primates are well adapted to foraging at height and make short work of reaching the flowers for the copiously produced sugar-rich nectar. As they visit, the lemurs get plenty of pollen on their snouts and surrounding fur, which is then spread to other flowers.

Following fertilisation capsular fruits are produced, and the capsules split open to display rows of indigo-blue seeds. To be accurate, the seeds themselves aren't blue, but are covered by blue arils. Blue is an unusual aril colour, but highly attractive to lemurs, and also to the nocturnal aye-aye (*Daubentonia madagascariensis*), another rare Madagascan endemic mammal. Aye-ayes are small primates known for their long, bushy tails, spidery fingers, big ears, and huge eyes that allow them to forage effectively in the dark. For years, scientists were at a loss to understand how the aye-aye could see the blue colour of the arils, as colour vision in mammals in the dark is presumed to be non-existent. As it turns out, however, compared with other primates, aye-ayes have enhanced vision in the blue range, allowing them to see this colour in dim light.

Like the tree's extraordinary pollination syndrome, the unusual details of its seed dispersal by aye-ayes is yet another example of co-evolution between Madagascar's endemic primates and its plants. The traveller's palm is not currently endangered or threatened, but populations of these charismatic primates are declining precipitously in their native habitats – the IUCN lists the aye-aye as Endangered and the lemur as Critically Endangered – and this has potentially profound consequences for the ecology of the traveller's palm in Madagascar.

WHITE
MULBERRY

Morus alba

Mulberries have a long and fascinating history in both the East and West. The genus consists of a dozen or so mostly similar looking, deciduous tree and shrub species native to warm temperate and subtropical regions in Asia, Africa and the Americas. All species have latex-producing stems and large, papery leaves that are prominently toothed and often irregularly lobed. This helps identify them as belonging to the fig family, Moraceae. The mulberries also have small, paired, thread-like stipules that accompany the leaves when they first emerge in the spring, but these are soon shed.

The edible mulberry is a soft, blackberry-like fruit with individual drupelets arranged along an elongated axis. Rather than the individual drupelets arising from a single flower as in blackberries and raspberries, each succulent drupelet in the mulberry is actually a separate fruit, derived from a separate flower. Once fertilised, the fruits expand and crowd together on the axis; hence, they are known as multiple fruits.

White mulberry is a fast-growing, short-lived, cold-hardy, small to medium-sized tree. The species is originally native to central and northern China, but is naturalised widely and cultivated in many places for the production of silk. The broad, rough-textured leaves are shiny green above and lighter below. Vigorous, stiff shoots typically bear irregularly lobed leaves, while older branches and especially reproductive stems carry smaller, mostly unlobed leaves. When not in leaf, white mulberry has few obvious distinguishing features, so may be difficult to recognise, but the trunks of older trees have scaly, attractively ridged light brown bark. The unisexual flowers are not particularly showy – the male flowers occur in small, elongated catkins and the females in more ovoid catkins. Most plants are either predominantly male or female, but some plants have both kinds of flowers and are self-fruitful. The fruitless (i.e. strictly male) selections of *M. alba* are often singled out for producing large amounts of wind-borne, allergenic pollen.

As an ornamental tree, white mulberry has a somewhat chequered history. In much of North America, it is nowadays considered a coarse, weedy tree, and in some jurisdictions has become invasive. White mulberry is easily grown, and like a willow even sprouts from thick branches hammered into the ground (one of the traditional propagation methods). The fruits are indeed messy – and the pavement-lifting abilities of mature trees legendary – but judging by the large number of selections still available, including both fruitless and fruitful cultivars, the tree must still have its champions. In Britain, reviews are generally more favourable, but that may be because the species is seldom cultivated here, at least in its natural guise. The common white mulberry in Britain is invariably the weeping and self-fruiting cultivar 'Pendula', which has stiff, stock-straight branches that hang like curtains.

The white mulberry fruit, which may be white, red or purple-black, is sweet-tasting, but considered insipid compared with the red mulberry (*M. rubra*) from the eastern US, and especially the black-fruited, black mulberry (*M. nigra*) from western Asia. The Romans took the black mulberry to Britain, both for its fruits and medicinal properties. The root bark of that species is renowned for expelling intestinal worms – a feature of the red mulberry as well, and a benefit arrived at independently by native Americans. However, it wasn't until Tudor times that black mulberry became a common culinary offering. Despite having tastier fruit, the black mulberry now generally takes a back seat to the white mulberry, both for its ornamental qualities and its production of leaves, which are the preferred food of the oriental silkworm.

The first mention of mulberries that most English-speakers remember is from the nursery rhyme that begins, 'Here we go round the mulberry bush/On a cold and frosty morning.' Notwithstanding that mulberries are trees, not bushes, the verse is thought to satirise attempts to establish a silk industry in Britain at various times between the sixteenth and nineteenth centuries, using black mulberry – while white mulberry is the favoured fodder for oriental silkworms, they *will* eat the leaves of black mulberry and produce silk, though it is of a coarser quality. Unfortunately, this period, known as the Little Ice Age, was a particularly difficult time to establish heat-loving trees in Great Britain, to say nothing of rearing caterpillars from China. Temperatures unsuited to the rearing of silkworms and the use of black mulberry leaves to feed them both probably contributed to the disappointing results.

Outside of cool temperate regions, the cultivation of *Morus alba* has always been inextricably linked with the production of silk. This is especially true of China, where the tree is originally native, and a number of different caterpillars naturally feed on the leaves. Just how long ago people learned that the cocoons of these moth larvae – silkworms in the vernacular – could be unravelled and spun into silk is widely debated. Many historians now believe that the technology for silk making was well understood as long ago as 4500 BCE.

The finest silk is said to be produced by the domestic silk moth (*Bombyx morii*) feeding on the semi-wilted leaves of white mulberry. The cocktail of chemicals in the mulberry's sticky latex combines perfectly with the *Bombyx* larva's own chemically rich saliva to produce an exceptional silk. The silk moth's domestication is known to have started with the wild silk moth (*B. mandarina*), a natural associate of the white mulberry. Selective breeding of the wild insect eventually rendered a slow-moving, flightless moth whose egg-laying could be effectively monitored and directed. And so moths that produced particularly large larvae that could produce correspondingly sizeable cocoons were chosen to improve the breeding lines. Now easily reared on wooden frames, silkworms could be kept well away from predators, and supplied and replenished with fresh mulberry leaves for as long as they were willing to eat them. Thus, generations of selective breeding produced large silkworms that, after a life munching on leaves, could supply a generous quantity of fine silken threads from their cocoons.

Like other moths and butterflies, when the larva of the domestic silk moth is at its largest, usually coinciding with the end of the growing season, it spins a protective cocoon and begins its metamorphosis as a pupa. The pupal case surrounds and protects the soon-to-be-moth's developing body and wings. When ready to emerge, the moth splits open its pupal case and produces silk-dissolving enzymes with which it creates an escape. It was soon discovered, however, that if the cocoons were first dropped into boiling water before the emerging moths had an opportunity to degrade the silk, the cocoons would be softened and the silk more easily unravelled. Various people have decried this aspect of silk production – Mahatma Gandhi, for one – as most of the silkworms are sacrificed, with only a few remaining to emerge and lay eggs for the next generation. While it might not satisfy ultra-strict vegetarians or virtuous Buddhists, people from many of the Asian cultures that practise silk-making actually consume the pupae after they are removed from the cocoons. In Yunnan, China, for example, the pupae are salted and fried with chili peppers, and in Thailand, they are processed and freeze-dried to make a crunchy, protein-rich snack.

Although Chinese rulers originally attempted to restrict silk production to within China's borders, the practice gradually took hold beyond its frontiers, and as silk commerce proliferated, trade routes grew. Famously, the Silk Road connected China and Southeast Asia with the Indian subcontinent, Persia, the Arabian Peninsula, east Africa and southern Europe. Fast-forward a few hundred years and silk production and white mulberries eventually reached the New World. Mexico still produces silk for domestic consumption, and Brazil is actually the fourth or fifth largest in worldwide production, but the American silk industry – never a thriving one – is no more. The legacy, however, is that white mulberry is a common tree, especially near to cities where plantations were originally established.

DAIMYO OR JAPANESE EMPEROR OAK

Quercus dentata

O aks are universal symbols of strength and longevity. The most common species are broad-crowned trees with tough, durable wood and lobed or coarsely toothed deciduous leaves as we have already seen; however, the genus comprises an enormous diversity of forms, from twiggy, small-leaved shrubs to tall, tropical forest evergreens. Of the 500 or so species, the majority are native to the drier parts of the Northern Hemisphere, represented by several areas of signif-icant diversity: eastern North America, south-western North America, Mexico, east Asia and the western and eastern Mediterranean regions. Regardless of whether they are dimin-utive shrubs, tropical giants, or the more familiar large deciduous trees of our parks and streets, all oaks have leaves that are alternately arranged on the branches, overwintering buds with often tiny, conspicuously overlapping scales, separate male and female wind-pollinated flowers in catkins, and acorns.

Anyone familiar with squirrels – either actual or animated – would easily recognise an acorn. The classic acorn consists of an ovoid nut anchored in a nest-like cup. The cup is made up of many, often tiny, overlapping scales. The acorn is unique to the oak. Other members of the oak family, Fagaceae, have a variety of different structures associated with their nuts. Some have husks that completely enclose the nuts – both the sweet chestnut (*Castanea sativa*) and common beech (*Fagus sylvatica*) feature this – but the chestnut husk is elaborated with sharp spines, while the beech has short, soft bristles. In daimyo oak the acorns are relatively small, with a hedgehog-like cup that bears long, bristly scales. Before the nut is fully developed the cup almost completely encases it, looking like a miniature sweet chestnut husk.

It is often said that the acorn is the fruit of an oak, but it is really just the nut that is the fruit. In the culinary vernacular, a fruit is something we might consider for dessert – an apple, melon or raspberry – but in the botanical sense a fruit is the ripened part of the flower that encloses developing seeds. Technically, it is an ovary, which contains ovules that, once fertilised, become seeds. In an oak, only a single seed usually develops in the ovary, and the ovary wall becomes hardened to form the nut. And acorns are edible, although some processing is needed to rid the starch-rich seeds of their natural tannins, otherwise they are too bitter and astringent to be palatable.

Prior to the introduction of wide-scale agriculture, many hunting-gathering people relied upon stored acorns for sustenance, especially during lean times. Acorn flour, which was mentioned by Pliny the Elder in his *Naturalis Historia* nearly 2,000 years ago and is now available for sale in trendier organic food markets in Europe and North America, can even be used to make bread. In Korea, the pulverised seeds of daimyo oak are soaked and repeatedly rinsed to remove the water-soluble tannins. The resultant paste is then dried and ready for partial rehydration to make an acorn jelly known as *dotori-muk*, or to make noodles for different versions of acorn noodle soup. In Korea this is known as *dotori-guksu*, and in Japan, *donguri-men*. Acorn meal is readily available in Korean groceries for those who are feeling adventurous. Daimyo acorn malt is also used to flavour beer in Korea and whisky in Japan.

Tannins, which are compounds present throughout the oak (and many other plants), are one of nature's most effective feeding deterrents. The concentration of tannins often determines the amount of leaf feeding by caterpillars, for example, and it is now widely understood that oaks and other trees can step up the production of tannins in their tissues in response to attacks by leaf-feeding insects. On the other hand, many animals have evolved the ability to tolerate acorn tannins, and squirrels and some birds typically cache large amounts underground for their winter larders. Those acorns that are not consumed but are left in the soil will often germinate and grow.

Daimyo oak is native to Japan, Korea and China and is classified as one of the white oaks. This is the largest group of cultivated oaks and consists of about 150 species, including both deciduous and evergreen species native across Europe, north Africa, North America, Central America, Mexico and east Asia. White oaks tend to have leaves with rounded lobes, and acorns that always ripen within the first year after forming. The cup of the acorn is usually composed of thickened, bumpy scales that are often embedded in a matrix of closely matted or fine hairs. The leaves of most white oaks are leathery and dull blue-green to glossy, dark green, and the bark mostly scaly or papery and seldom deeply furrowed, but with daimyo oak, the bark is ruggedly corrugated and corky and develops deep, vertical furrows with age.

A small, sparsely and stoutly branched tree, daimyo oak often has exceptionally large – frequently foot-long – dark-green leaves, by far its most conspicuous feature. In Japan, the ample size, attractively sinuous edge ornamentation and suppleness of the young leaves makes them ideal as the wrappers for traditional *kashiwa-mochi* (red-bean-filled rice-cakes) for *Kodomo-no-hi* (Children's Day) on 5 May. Often described as lyre-shaped in outline, the leaves are narrow at the base, gradually broadening toward the tip, and have undulating lobes or broad 'teeth' along the margins (*dentata* means 'toothed'). On a young tree the enormous leaves can look almost ridiculously outsized and the soft hairs that often coat the leaf-backs make them extraordinary to the touch. They are a wonder at any time.

Like common beech, deciduous oaks, including daimyo oak, are notorious for marcescence – the retention of dry, partially withered leaves throughout autumn and winter. Instead of a more or less synchronised leaf fall, a marcescent tree will often drop leaves periodically through the winter, with a final dump as buds begin to swell in the early spring.

For those whose job it is to clean up leaves in a garden, such a feature can be somewhat annoying, especially with leaves as large as those of the daimyo oak.

Some people find marcescent trees unattractive, and the continuous soft, raspy rattle of their dried leaves in the wind can be grating. Once trees become reproductively mature, however, the acorn-bearing branches are generally free of leaves in winter.

CURIOUSER AND CURIOUSER

Trees are poems that the earth writes upon the sky.

KHALIL GIBRAN

Sometimes, what connects a group of plants is what doesn't unite them. Each of the plants in this chapter has a separate story to tell. Each belongs to a different branch on the tree of life and for all of them, the terms 'unusual' or 'unexpected' can be equally applied. Boxleaf azara's leaves are not what they appear to be. Similarly, the celery top pine has leaves that aren't edible, nor are they even leaves at all, while those of makrut lime are definitely leafy (and edible), but they also make you see double. Falconer's rhododendron is a proper forest tree with more than one compelling attribute, in addition to its enormously tall stems. The asuhi cypress, another Asian forest inhabitant, has a few surprises up its reptilian sleeves, particularly for dallying insects and curious leaf turners. There's not much different about the magnificent giant dogwood, except that its buds are avowedly non-conforming. Speaking of renegades, the leaves of Virginia round-leaf birch trees are as deliciously, intoxicatingly different as they are rare.

BOXLEAF
AZARA

Azara microphylla

F
ew trees in temperate gardens come from South America.
The vast majority of ornamental trees in our gardens –
maples, oaks, ashes, birches, locusts and the like – originate in
Asia, Europe or eastern North America. South America has
few habitats that both provide winter cold and conditions
suitable for growing trees. Only in the Andes mountains and
near the southern tip of South America, in Patagonia, are there
are places we might deem as climatically similar to where other,
more familiar garden trees grow. Even here, conditions are not
always ideal, and as a result South American trees are just not
that commonly cultivated. But there is one notable exception
– and many readers will have already cottoned on to this; that
is, the monkey puzzle tree (*Araucaria araucana* see page 195),
a magnificent, if somewhat unusual-looking, conifer.

Monkey puzzle has a range that covers a small part of the same territory as species in the genus *Azara*. There are some ten different azaras, all attractive evergreen shrubs and trees, but only a scant few are well known, as the majority need practically frost-free conditions. Boxleaf azara, also known as *chin-chin* where it grows in the wild, is the cold-hardiest. It is an 8-metre-tall tree native to shaded mountain slopes in the Andes of south-central Chile and Argentina. Boxleaf azara is usually a small, multi-stemmed tree with dark brown, flaky bark and a rounded, dense, fine-textured crown of layered branches, closely set on the main stems. Each lateral branch has an almost herringbone pattern of horizontal secondary branches, much like in the common rockspray cotoneaster (*Cotoneaster horizontalis*). In shaded plants, the leaves lie flat and the stems spread out, producing especially broad tiers. Throughout, the slender shoots are generously clothed in fingernail-sized and smaller, forward-pointing, glossy, dark green, box-like leaves (*microphylla* means 'small leaf'). Each leaf has a few tiny marginal teeth that are mostly partly obscured by the recurved, wavy margin, and a depressed midrib that gives the leaves a little reflective lift.

Perhaps surprisingly, azaras are members of the willow family, Salicaceae. Until recently they were assigned to a family of mostly tropical plants with un-willow-like, showy, insect-pollinated flowers, but that family has now been folded into Salicaceae. The placement of azaras alongside the willows and poplars acknowledges a similar chemistry and a few common, though not very obvious, morphological character-istics. Salicin, which was traditionally harvested from willow bark and, famously, chemically modified to produce aspirin (acetylsalicylic acid), is also present in *Azara*. The Mapuche, an indigenous people inhabiting the north-west Patagonian Andes, are known to use boxleaf azara for its analgesic and anti-inflammatory properties, probably in much the same way that Northern-Hemisphere first peoples use willow bark.

One of the morphological features azaras share with willows is the presence of salicoid teeth on the margins of its leaves. These specialised teeth are found throughout the family and characterised by small, hard points that are fused to the tooth apex. More interesting, perhaps, is that the tooth-points function as secretory glands. Both anti-feedant aromatic resins (e.g. in poplars) and nectars with high sugar content for attracting insects have been identified from the salicoid teeth of different species in the family.

A somewhat more conspicuous feature shared by members of Salicaceae is the frequent presence of stipules. In willows, stipules often take the form of small symmetrical pairs of leafy green flaps or flanges that accompany the base of the petiole, where it meets the stem – the jagged leafy outgrowths at the base of the petioles of long-stemmed roses might be a more familiar example. Stipules have various functions in the plant world, including as protection for unexpanded leaves in the buds of certain plants, such as magnolias (see page 209) and tulip trees (see page 21). Many plants, notably species in the pea family, have stipules that persist and become spinose – that is, sharp and hardened – such that they act to protect branches as well as leaves from browsing animals. The green-briars (*Smilax* species) have stipules that become tendrils, which allow the plants to climb. The best understood function of stipules is the photosynthetic one in which the azaras excel.

In most plants, stipules are generally shed before the leaves mature, but in the azaras they persist and are foliose, with a texture indistinguishable from that of the leaves. In general, azara stipules are nearly round. A close look at the stems of *A. microphylla* reveals one large, rounded, forward-pointing leaf, opposite a half-sized, rounded stipule, angled jauntily backward on the stem. The overall effect is unusual and attractive, although it requires more than a superficial scrutiny to make out the subtle patterning. There are few examples of this phenomenon in the plant world, where a stipule both takes the form and adopts the function of a persisting leaf.

In early spring, usually February or March, small clusters of golden-yellow flowers, barely more than one millimetre across, break from miniature, rounded red buds in the axils of the leaves. Although visually insignificant, the flowers to some people smell marvellously of vanilla or chocolate, and are produced abundantly all along the youngest shoots of mature plants, though they are mostly hidden by the glossy leaves. Most gardeners cultivate boxleaf azara primarily for these delightfully fragrant, early spring flowers, but the longer-lasting foliar offerings of this diminutive tree are arguably more attractive. The genus is named for either Felix de Azara (1742–1821), Spanish naturalist, geographer and writer who spent time in South America or, more probably, his brother, José Nicholás (1730–1804), diplomat and Spanish patron of the arts and sciences, who did not.

VIRGINIA ROUND-LEAVED BIRCH

Betula lenta f. *uber*

The birches, belonging to the genus *Betula*, are some of our most familiar temperate trees, occurring in forests across North America, Europe and Asia and most often found in cool mountainous areas. *Betula* is also the one of the most northerly, deciduous tree genera, with a circumboreal distribution, growing up to the treeline in places, or until it is replaced by evergreen, coniferous species. They are noted for being a pioneer species, colonising areas in the wake of some form of disturbance, either natural of unnatural – as likely as you are to see a birch growing on the lava fields of a volcano, in many areas they are also the first tree you'll notice growing in abandoned urban places such as old car parks or industrial areas. Their tiny, winged, wind-dispersed seeds are most efficient in finding small cracks and crevices to take root in.

The leaves of most birches tend to be more or less ovate and relatively unspectacular, though the yellow autumn colour of some of the species competes with that of other members of the birch family, which includes hornbeams (*Carpinus*) and hazels (*Corylus*). Birches are also noted for their bark, with several species exhibiting spectacularly white, sometimes peeling stems. Other species are darker and perhaps less charismatic, though their trunks have distinctive, horizontal lenticels – sites of gas exchange – which are long and narrow.

The Virginia round-leaved birch may be one of these less showy species, though it has one of the most interesting leaves and intriguing histories of all the birches. Discovered in 1914 growing in Cressy Creek, Smyth County, Virginia, the tree was initially thought to be a variety of a birch native to the area, *Betula lenta*, but being so different it was eventually elevated to species rank in 1945. Where a plant species is determined to be new to science, or when a plant is deemed important for further study, a representative sample of the specimen is pressed and dried, then attached to a standardised sheet of paper and labelled with the collector's name and a description of the collecting site. Dried, pressed plants for scientific study are stored in specialised, climate-controlled rooms known as herbaria, and the sheets are called herbarium specimens or vouchers. The birch's original herbarium speci-men shows slender branchlets holding small, rounded leaves, with four to five secondary veins, heart-shaped bases and small, sharply serrated margins, and it was solely from this voucher that the plant was known for more than 60 years, until another wild specimen was collected in 1974. And it wasn't for lack of trying. Several attempts were made to re-find and collect this curious birch and the fact that it took over 60 years highlights that even in well-known, highly populated and documented areas, there are new discoveries waiting to be made.

Since 1974 it has been well studied, though has still only ever been found in small populations along Cressy Creek, its rarity being due not only to local agricultural pressures but also to a quirk of the plant itself. Rather than being a genetically stable species, the Virginia round-leaved birch is a mutant form of *Betula lenta,* the sweet or cherry birch, that occurs only once in every 100 seedlings raised. This discovery was only made earlier this century and prior to this the plant's uniqueness and scarcity led to the formation of the *Betula uber* Protection, Management and Research Coordinating Committee; it was also the first tree to be protected under the US Endangered Species Act. Actions taken in accordance with this saw its population increase, though it has subsequently decreased and, given its mutant status, it seems destined to remain rare. However, efforts to conserve this botanical oddity mean it is now well represented in temperate botanic gardens in Europe and North America.

Along with its distinct leaf shape, the Virginia round-leaf birch is notable for the presence of large amounts of methyl salicylate, or oil of wintergreen, in its stems, buds and leaves. Its presence is evident when stems are rubbed or bruised, exuding a strong scent immediately reminiscent of sports changing rooms; the chemical has anti-inflammatory properties and is a common component of therapeutic muscle rubs, creams and ointments, as well as toothpastes and chewing gums. It is also the primary constituent of birch essential oil, used in aromatherapy.

Methyl salicylate occurs in all birches and indeed most land plants in some volume, with large amounts also found in more than a dozen other birches as well as shrubs known as wintergreens, so named for the chemical, and belonging to the genus *Gaultheria*. Derived from salicylic acid, its presence appears to help fight infection and disease, and levels within plants are often increase in response to stress or injury. It is a volatile compound, emitted as a gas, and evidence suggests that its emission may be used by plants to signal danger to other plants, or even other parts of the same plant that trigger disease resistance and the activation of genes crucial to defence.

If you're not sure whether or not something is a birch, scent can therefore also provide an identification aid. Though the Virginia round-leaved birch is distinctive enough, several other species are morphologically similar, but often less pungent, and knowing where to rub can help head you in the right direction.

FALCONER'S RHODODENDRON

Rhododendron falconeri

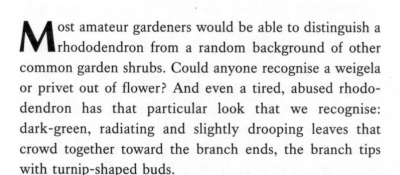

Most amateur gardeners would be able to distinguish a rhododendron from a random background of other common garden shrubs. Could anyone recognise a weigela or privet out of flower? And even a tired, abused rhododendron has that particular look that we recognise: dark-green, radiating and slightly drooping leaves that crowd together toward the branch ends, the branch tips with turnip-shaped buds.

It's no wonder rhododendrons are familiar plants, as the genus is one of the most species-rich in cultivation. With more than 1,000 species, *Rhododendron* is distributed in montane to alpine habitats across the temperate Northern Hemisphere, especially throughout the mountain ranges of Asia and even reaching into the subtropics, as far south as northern Australia.

And as far as garden hybrids of rhododendrons go, those are nearly countless.

In some places, primarily the Himalayas and the mountains of south-western China, rhododendrons can become sizeable trees. Falconer's rhododendron (*Rhododendron falconeri*) is one such species, and is native to the extraordinarily biodiverse eastern Himalayan region that includes parts of India, Nepal and Bhutan. Observing the substantial bulk of a mature Falconer's rhododendron, one cannot help but be impressed. Branches of this stately tree are stout and strong, and the mature stems are covered in loose, rough, red-brown bark that flakes off to expose a smooth, lighter-coloured under-bark. The magnificent paddle-like leaves are leathery and thick, and finely wrinkled above. Like other rhododendrons, the leaves are borne in radiating clusters at the tips of the branches, but the back of each leaf of Falconer's rhododendron is coated in a suede-like pelt of warm, rusty-brown hairs. Looking up through a mature specimen, the effect can be glorious. Enormous, rounded clusters of huge, creamy-white to yellow, fragrant flowers top off the leaf rosettes in late spring. The flowers are also noteworthy beyond their size and number, as they are reputed to be among the longest-lasting of any that rhododendrons produce.

Remarkable as cultivated trees might be, they are nothing compared with those in the wild. Small forests of centuries-old *R. falconeri* still occur in the Himalayas. Whether in pure stands of 15-metre-tall specimens or isolated pockets of giants exceeding 25 metres in height, this species, especially when capped with yellow, elicits awe, if not poetry, from any who witness it.

Indumentum is the term for the persisting hairy vestiture

that occurs on the leaves, stems and stalks of rhododendrons. A degree of hairiness is common on almost all emerging shoots, but the hairs are typically shed from leaf tops well before the leaves have finished expanding. Some forms of Falconer's rhododendron are known for the indumentum that persists for an extended time on the upper side of the leaves. These plants, known as *R. falconeri* subsp. *eximium*, are truly exquisite. Aptly, *eximium* means 'distinguished' or 'choice'. But why indumentum occurs on some high-elevation species and not others is somewhat mysterious, as it is clearly beneficial. Not surprisingly, the felted hairs – like a fur coat – provide insulation to new, emerging growth in the spring. The hairs also prevent feeding by herbivores (who wants a mouthful of hair?) and provide some summer shade if situated on the upper leaf surface.

What is not widely known is that the presence or absence and specific types of hairs on a rhododendron leaf are important features in differentiating groups of species. Some rhododendrons have an indumentum that is composed of single, unbranched hairs that stand erect; others have hairs that are so short, fine and dense that they don't look like hairs at all, but like a painted surface. The group to which Falconer's rhododendron belongs is characterised by hairs that are branched and cup- or goblet-shaped and that stand above a primary layer of much shorter hairs. Any sort of leaf hair is technically known as a trichome. In rhododendrons, they can be large or small, thick or thin, hair-like or branched (like split ends), or flattened and scale-like. As the Falconer's rhododendron leaf ages and the longer red-brown hairs of indumentum are shed, lighter-coloured hairs of the lower stratum become agglutinated (stuck together), creating a thin, unbroken skin over the leaf. Some magnification is usually required to see these coatings or the individual hairs in detail, but the indumentum of many rhododendrons is like felted wool or velvet, or springy, like a marshmallow coating, and these are easily characterised by touch alone. Glandular trichomes are specialised hairs that are bulbous and filled with liquid – usually an irritating or poisonous compound, often pleasantly aromatic. Glands and gland-tipped hairs are common in rhododendrons, especially around the reproductive parts of the flowers, and they provide a greater level of feeding deterrence than hairs alone. Each ovary in the Falconer's rhododendron flower is covered in glands, but these are found nowhere else on the plant.

The earliest European to formally describe *R. falconeri* was Joseph Dalton Hooker, an English explorer and botanist and good friend of Charles Darwin. Hooker was the first scientist to catalogue rhododendrons in the Himalayas and did so in 1849. He named the species after the Scottish naturalist, Hugh Falconer, who only a few years prior had studied the flora, fauna and geology of much of the same area that Hooker explored. Accounts by plant explorers, from Hooker to the present day, speak of being humbled by the size and beauty of staggeringly huge specimens of Falconer's and other Himalayan rhododendrons.

CELERY-TOP PINE

Phyllocladus aspleniifolius

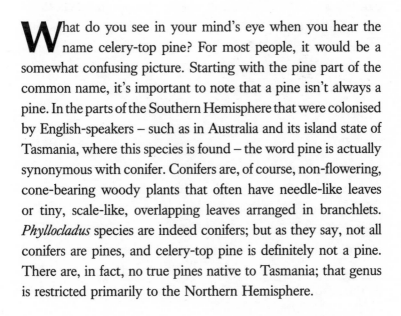

What do you see in your mind's eye when you hear the name celery-top pine? For most people, it would be a somewhat confusing picture. Starting with the pine part of the common name, it's important to note that a pine isn't always a pine. In the parts of the Southern Hemisphere that were colonised by English-speakers – such as in Australia and its island state of Tasmania, where this species is found – the word pine is actually synonymous with conifer. Conifers are, of course, non-flowering, cone-bearing woody plants that often have needle-like leaves or tiny, scale-like, overlapping leaves arranged in branchlets. *Phyllocladus* species are indeed conifers; but as they say, not all conifers are pines, and celery-top pine is definitely not a pine. There are, in fact, no true pines native to Tasmania; that genus is restricted primarily to the Northern Hemisphere.

The 'celery-top' part of the name is purely descriptive, and fairly accurately depicts the look of *Phyllocladus aspleniifolius*, as well as other species in the genus. The scientific name *aspleniifolius* refers to the uncanny likeness of the foliage to the fronds of some ferns – specifically, spleenworts (*Asplenium* species). In particular, they closely resemble those of the tiny European wall spleenwort, *A. ruta-muraria*, although it could be argued that the leaflets of celery (*Apium graveolens*) are a better match for size. On the off-chance that a gardener might consider adding celery-top pine to soup (as one might a celery-top), it should be stressed that all parts of *Phyllocladus* trees are poisonous.

In the celery-top pine, the foliage is not what most people think it is. The broad, green, leaf-like, photosynthetic organs of the tree are not leaves, but flattened branches called cladodes or phylloclades (which is the derivation of the genus name). While unique among the conifers, cladodes are widely known and represented in a range of flowering plant families. The leafy segmented stems of the Christmas cactus (*Schlumbergera* species) are cladodes, as are the delicate 'leaves' of the asparagus fern (*Asparagus setaceus*), for example. Cladodes were once thought to be merely modified, flattened branches, but they are now more accurately interpreted as being intermediate between leaves and branches, displaying features of both. For the most part, each of the celery-top pine's crowded shoots are terminated by flattened cladodes, which are either irregularly lobed or further divided into a compound structure, with secondary cladodes alternating to either side of a central axis. At the base of each shoot and often also scattered along the edges of the cladodes are true leaves, though these are reduced to tiny vestigial scales. They are red in colour, like the emerging shoots, but are usually quickly shed and often go unnoticed. Seedling plants also bear apparently normal, needle-like leaves before they transition to producing cladodes. A third type of leaf – green and thread-like – accompanies the base of the stalks that carry the male and female cones.

The plum yew family, Podocarpaceae, to which the five *Phyllocladus* species belong, is the second largest of the conifers, and enormously diverse. While not strictly a Southern Hemisphere family, Podocarpaceae are much less common north of the equator – rather like the true pines in reverse. And like the monkey puzzles, the podocarps did most of their early diversification in Gondwana, the former southern supercontinent that began splitting apart 180 million years ago. This is why, in part, their centres of diversity are in the Southern Hemisphere. Podocarps range in size from miniature alpines to subtropical rainforest giants. As conifers go, the family produces the greatest diversity and arguably the most interesting of cones. But to be accurate, podocarp cones aren't really very cone-like at all.

Seed plants, including conifers, produce stamens that bear pollen, and ovules that, once fertilised by that pollen, produce seeds. In conifers, the ovule is always borne on a modified scale, which, in the more familiar conifers, is usually sandwiched between a series of tightly overlapping or tight-fitting scales that form a woody cone, such as one would see in a pine or cypress. In podocarps, there are usually only a few minute, ovule-bearing scales borne on tiny stalks. The scales are inverted so that they provide a protective covering for the ovule. Once the ovule is fertilised, the scale enlarges, forming a covering for the seed known as an epimatium. The epimatium may be thin, or leathery and thick, and is often coloured. At the same time, a set of tiny bracts below the ovule-bearing scale fuse with the stalk and enlarge to become the carpidium, a fleshy and often brightly coloured structure.

In terms of cones, the celery pines go one further than other podocarps, in producing a white, sweet-tasting, oil-rich body known as an aril that partially covers the seed. Researchers are not in agreement as to whether the aril is an enlarged modified epimatium or something else altogether. The aril, and the black-green seed at its centre, provide a striking contrast to the red carpidium below. Arils are, by and large, bird-attracting tackle, and familiar to many as the fleshy, seed-enclosing structures of yew (*Taxus* species). Because of arils in both genera, some early researchers thought the yews and celery pines were closely related, but they are not. In fact, they belong to different families whose ancestral populations diverged around 250 million years ago. Continuing with the theme of unusual structures, celery-top pine produces both its pollen and seed-cones at the base of the shoots, but also often dotted along the edges of the cladodes, reminding us that these flattened structures are as much stem as leaf.

The celery pines, as the genus *Phyllocladus* is generally known, are mostly upland tropical and temperate rainforest trees, with species native to New Zealand, Tasmania and Malesia, including Papua New Guinea, Borneo, India and the Philippines. Celery-top pine is not the largest of its genus – that distinction goes to one of the tropical species – but it is a long-lived timber tree, often growing to more than 20 metres in height, that has been harvested for its attractive, aromatic wood for centuries. Commercial logging has, unfortunately, been more or less restricted to the diminishing supply of old-growth individuals, and this does not bode well for the survival of this fascinating conifer.

ASUHI CYPRESS

Thujopsis dolobrata

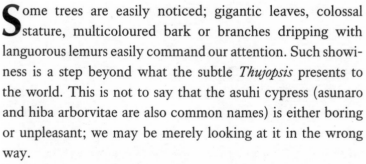

Some trees are easily noticed; gigantic leaves, colossal stature, multicoloured bark or branches dripping with languorous lemurs easily command our attention. Such showiness is a step beyond what the subtle *Thujopsis* presents to the world. This is not to say that the asuhi cypress (asunaro and hiba arborvitae are also common names) is either boring or unpleasant; we may be merely looking at it in the wrong way.

The genus *Thujopsis* is part of the cypress family, Cupressaceae, and asuhi cypress is one of twenty conifer species that are found exclusively in Japan. Of those endemic conifers, a small number are so celebrated for the value of their timber that they are used in temple construction, hinoki (*Chamaecyparis obtusa*) being the most valued. Asuhi cypress is considered excellent construction timber. The fragrant yellow wood is both easily worked and strong, and is even used under water as it has considerable rot-resisting properties, but it doesn't quite make the grade with Japanese artisans. In fact, the name asunaro is short for *asu wa hinoki ni narou*, which is a mildly disparaging 'let's become hinoki tomorrow'.

Asuhi cypress is similar in form to other shade-adapted cypress relatives, with a dense conical crown to 20 or 30 metres tall, and a wide skirt of branches that often persists for decades all the way to the ground. The branches of asuhi cypress tend to describe strong arcs, descending then ascending, with the coarse, heavy foliage drooping along the main part of the branch, then narrowing toward the tip. Much like that of other cypresses, the bark is dark chestnut-brown, fibrous and vertically furrowed. Lower branches commonly layer themselves in the duff and gradually produce multiple uprights around the main stem. Such trees appear like isolated islands in the landscape. Asuhi cypress is the only species in the genus, but its leaves are surprisingly similar to a number of other cypress relatives, including *Chamaecyparis* (false cypress) and especially *Thuja* (arborvitae). *Thujopsis* means 'like a *Thuja*'.

Members of Cupressaceae are easily identified by the characteristic aromas of their wood and crushed foliage, and a wide variety of aromatic compounds have been identified in asuhi cypress. As in other species, these volatile compounds confer anti-feedant and antifungal qualities, but they can also smell wonderful. In Japan, oil extracted from the wood is prized for its sweet, slightly smoky fragrance. It is used in both aromatherapy for its relaxing properties and as an insect repellent. Even asuhi sawdust has been shown to deter caterpillars. Notably, when spread around the base of another Japanese conifer, the Japanese black pine (*Pinus thunbergii*), the sawdust has a larvacidal effect on the destructive pine needle gall midge (*Thecodiplosis japonensis*). The compound responsible is carvacrol, which is also known as oregano oil. Carvacrol is found in a range of plants including, not surprisingly, oregano, and is widely noted for its antifungal, antibacterial and insect-repelling properties.

As in most other cypress relatives, separate male and female reproductive structures are borne on the same individual tree. Both the asuhi cypress's small, ephemeral, dark brown pollen-cones and the sturdier, waxy-blue seed-cones are produced singly at the tips of short lateral branchlets on the outer branchlet sprays. Cupressaceous genera are readily differentiated on the basis of their reproductive structures – those of *Thujopsis* are distinctive – but a closer look at the leaves provides some significant contrasts, as well.

Most cypresses produce overlapping, flattened scale leaves, the green scales seldom more than a few millimetres in length. They clothe the shoot tips completely and the shoots are either arranged with a radial phyllotaxy, as in the true cypresses, or organised in large, flattened, frond- or fan-shaped clusters, known as branchlet sprays. The flattened branchlet spray is an adaptation to shaded environments, common to forest-dwelling cypresses. Although composed of hundreds of individual scale leaves, the sprays are essentially leaf-like, providing an almost equivalent amount of photosynthetic surface as a contiguous leaf of the same dimensions. Leaves are long-lived but, because the scales are tightly overlapping, cannot be shed individually when they finally start to break down. Again, like other cypresses, whole branchlet sprays are shed, in a process known as cladoptosis.

Juvenile growth in asuhi cypress seedlings is markedly

different from the scale-like, flattened growth of adult plants. Seedling leaves are spirally arranged, generally narrow, some- what curved and sharp-pointed, and they stick out from the stem. These give way to flattened, adult leaves relatively early, and this expression of heterophylly – i.e. differently shaped and arranged juvenile and adult leaves – is well expressed in most cypresses.

In asuhi cypress, like the aforementioned genera, the scales on the adult sprays are arranged in pairs along the stems, with each successive pair borne at right angles to the pair imme- diately below. This four-ranked leaf pattern is known as a decussate arrangement and is common throughout the plant kingdom, as it is an efficient way to maximise leaf area while preventing self-shading. The pairs on the broad, facial surface of the branchlet spray are flat, while those along the sides are folded around the shoot and appear hatchet-shaped in outline (*dolobra* means 'hatchet-shaped'). Regardless of their position, each pair overlaps the pair below. This creates a regular geom- etry interrupted only by individual branches that alternate along the stems. Close inspection of the sprays of any of these genera reveals the same pattern.

The branches of asuhi cypress splay more widely and stiffly than those of *Thuja*, but the difference in texture is usually apparent only when viewed at close range. Compared with other cypresses with flattened branchlet sprays, the lateral leaves of asuhi cypress are about three times as large, and more spreading, with the tips diverging markedly from the stem. All of the scales, both facial and lateral, are similarly large. The two types are conspicuously thick and ridged on the upper side of the branchlet spray, glossy dark green and minutely pebbled. There is something reptilian about the size and texture of the scaly leaves, and indeed one common name for asuhi is 'lizard tree'.

The decussate nature of the leaves is conspicuous on the branchlets, but especially so on any vigorous upright shoot. These are pencil-thick and marked beautifully by the patterned arrangement of sharply up-pointed symmetrical leaves and the corky brown bark that frames them. Perhaps the most outstanding feature of the tree is the least obvious. Turning a branchlet spray over reveals broad white-waxy patches in the hollows on the lateral leaves, as well as waxy stripes in the furrows on the facial leaves. These waxy deposits not only contrast starkly with the deep green of the scales, but magnify and make plain the beauty of the unexpected leaf geometry hidden in plain sight.

TABLE DOGWOOD

Cornus controversa

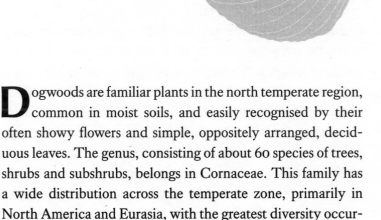

Dogwoods are familiar plants in the north temperate region, common in moist soils, and easily recognised by their often showy flowers and simple, oppositely arranged, deciduous leaves. The genus, consisting of about 60 species of trees, shrubs and subshrubs, belongs in Cornaceae. This family has a wide distribution across the temperate zone, primarily in North America and Eurasia, with the greatest diversity occurring in China. Both the scientific and common names are etymologically related: *Cornus* from Latin *cornu* = horn (i.e. hard, like animal horn), and dogwood from Old English *dagge* + wood (a dag is a hard peg or skewer).

The hard wood is so dense that it does not float. Especially prior to the Industrial Revolution, the wood was widely used for tool handles, pegs, spools and weapons – spears and bows, primarily – but nowadays the wood is prized for a variety of turned objects, and because of its density and superior shock resistance dogwood is also used for golf-club heads, textile shuttles and mallet heads.

Table dogwood is a wide-spreading tree of up to 20 metres tall, native across much of temperate Japan, China, Indochina and the Himalayas. It is a tall, deciduous species with an attractively tiered growth habit shared with few other dogwoods. Trees have smooth, grey, mostly unadorned bark. New shoots are purplish to purplish-green, then green with conspicuous, rounded lenticels and semicircular leaf scars, before becoming obscured with yellowish-grey bark. Among *Cornus* species, only the western North American Pacific dogwood (*C. nuttallii*) is taller, but the branch spread of table dogwood is often exceptionally wide – to 15 metres or more – making it the broadest of all the taller species (hence the common names table dogwood and giant dogwood).

Cornus leaves are all surprisingly similar; it is often difficult to differentiate species by their leaves alone. Many are about the same size and roughly oval with a rounded base and pointed tip, and the margins are always untoothed and typically undulate – i.e. the edges are wavy, interrupting the normal flat plane of the leaf. Dogwood leaves also share a characteristic vein architecture, where the lateral veins all curve attractively toward the leaf apex. Both the primary midvein and the arcuate lateral veins are always impressed above and prominent below. Incredibly, these characteristics carry over all species, from the diminutive, herbaceous, dwarf cornels to the shrubby osiers and the tree dogwoods. An interesting trick and reliable identification feature for the genus can be performed with the leaves of any dogwood. A leaf that is carefully torn though the middle will remain connected by tiny elastic threads. The leaves of table dogwood look much

like those of a number of species, but colour more spectacularly than most other dogwoods, taking on reds, oranges and
especially purples in the autumn. They are used in folk medicine and are reputed to relieve pain and reduce swelling, but
little about their chemistry has been studied.

Like most plants, dogwoods are differentiated on the basis
of their flowers and fruits, and from this perspective the major
dogwood groups, if not the species, are usually more clearly
distinguishable. Dogwood flowers are small, usually less than
5 millimetres across, but there are two basic inflorescence
types. The tiny flowers are either aggregated and condensed
into a button-like head, and subtended by a showy set of
white bracts – these are the most familiar tree dogwoods – or
they occur separately in more or less flattened inflorescences.
The osier dogwoods, common plants along wetland margins,
with often brightly coloured stems, produce their white
flowers in flattened clusters. Table dogwood is closest to this
group, which makes it somewhat unusual, at least when
compared with the more familiar, cultivated tree dogwoods.
En masse the flowers have considerable charm, particularly
when viewed from above.

Another defining feature of table dogwood is their alternately arranged buds. This is the derivation of its scientific
name, *C. controversa*. Not conforming to the typical opposite
arrangement was apparently controversial when the tree was
first named. Were it not for the remarkably similar-looking
eastern North American pagoda dogwood (*C. alternifolia*),
which also has an alternate arrangement, table dogwood would
be unique in the genus.

Along with leaf arrangement, table dogwood and pagoda
dogwood share the distinctive layered habit that gives them

their common names. Both have white flowers in flattened clusters followed by small, oil-rich, blue-black berries that are quickly taken by marauding birds in the autumn. As they are presumed to share a common ancestor from some-time prior to the break-up of the North American and Eurasian continental masses some fifty-five million years ago, the two are considered vicariant (sister) species. Not surprisingly, a few changes have taken place between the two in the intervening years. In particular, table dogwood is a sizeable tree, while pagoda dogwood is twiggy and usually shrub-like. Table dogwood shows a greater resistance to the soil-borne disease known as verticillium wilt, an all-too-common scourge in Western gardens. The leaves, too, although superficially similar, have a significant distinction. Much in the same way as the American and Chinese tulip trees (another vicariant pair), the Asian table dogwood and Chinese tulip tree are endowed with papillae, nearly micro-scopic, ball-bearing-like protuberances, on the backs of the leaves. Their American counterparts have none (see tulip tree, page 21).

Finally, it's worth noting that the most horticulturally popular manifestation of the table dogwood – at least in the West – is a selection with variegated leaves. Although the wild species is highly ornamental, it is seldom seen in gardens. Instead, *C. controversa* 'Variegata' (wedding cake tree) is preferred. It has smaller-than-normal cream-edged leaves and a slower rate of growth than the species. Established trees produce well-spaced horizontal layers of purplish stems lavishly spread with creamy-white foliage. So deliciously confection-like, the trees are endlessly sought after by the gardening elite.

The leaf variegation, a celebrated phenomenon, is caused by an infection by a plant virus or a phytoplasma (a bacterial parasite). Either way, the infection prevents the leaf from manufacturing the usual number of chloroplasts in the places where they usually reside. Photosynthetic potential is thus reduced, but then colours other than green – mostly white and yellow, but also red tints – can come to the fore. Consistent malformation of especially the edges and tips of the leaves is a reliable sign that plants are infected with a virus or phytoplasma, as are variable degrees of variegation among those leaves. Genetic mutations are another common cause of variegation, but they seldom come with correspondingly distorted leaves. The wedding cake tree is a classic example of the former; all the leaves are oddly shaped and are in varying degrees of whiteness. Were this not sufficiently showy, come autumn, under sunny conditions, red and bubblegum-pink hues are incorporated into the mix. With this tree even wild-species purists can have their cake.

MAKRUT LIME

Citrus hystrix

Supermarkets are excellent places to botanise. Away from seasonal cut-flower selections and ever-expanding house-plant sections, the fresh produce gives a wealth of opportunity to become more familiar with numerous plant families. Apples (*Malus*) and pears (*Pyrus*) belong to the rose family, Rosaceae; parsnip (*Pastinaca*) and celery (*Apium*) are members of the carrot family, Apiaceae; endive (*Cichorium*) and lettuce (*Lactuca*) belong to the daisy family, Asteraceae; cauliflower and broccoli (both *Brassica*) to the cabbage or mustard family, Brassicaceae; and spinach (*Spinacia*) and beets (*Beta*) to the amaranth family, Amaranthaceae. And then the familiar array of citrus fruits – lemons, limes and oranges, all belonging to the genus *Citrus*, in the rue family, Rutaceae.

As well as citrus fruits, one of the most popular citrus products is the leaves of *Citrus hystrix*, a small tree native to parts of tropical regions of China and Southeast Asia, and widely introduced to other tropical regions. Often sold as 'kaffir lime', this name derives from the Arabic *kafir*, which translates as 'non-Muslim' and was used by Arab sailors in reference to indigenous peoples of Africa. It was later adopted by Portuguese sailors and later by Dutch and British settlers, particularly in South Africa. Though it has been viewed as a racial slur since the nineteenth century, and its usage was criminalised in South Africa in the 1970s, its widespread use in the Northern Hemisphere has persisted. Makrut lime, or simply makrut, the name used in Thailand and elsewhere, is preferred and thus used here.

Makrut lime leaves are hugely popular for flavouring in Southeast Asian, particularly Thai, cooking. Strongly aromatic, smelling of a combination of lemon, lime and mandarin orange, the fresh leaves are either torn or chopped and used as a spice, as well as a digestive aid. Rich in essential oils, among the leaf's many benefits are its antimicrobial, antioxidant and antimicrobial properties. They are widely used in traditional medicine to treat ailments including headache, flu and fevers, while rubbing fresh leaves on teeth and gums is reputed to be beneficial for dental health.

Significant to the leaves' curative qualities is the primary compound found within them, citronellal, which is also responsible for the familiar citrus scent so apparent when makrut lime leaves and those of other *Citrus* plants are crushed. *Citrus* leaves are not, however, the main source of citronella oil, which is derived from lemongrass, *Cymbopogon*, in the grass family, Poaceae. Citronellal is also present, to varying degrees, in numerous other plants including some Australian members of the myrtle family, such as the aptly named lemon-scented tea tree (*Leptospermum petersonii*) and lemon-scented gum (*Corymbia citriodora*).

As with the eucalypts, the source of the makrut lime's essential oils is secretory glands present throughout the leaf. These are in fact a character of most species in the rue family but are particularly prominent in *Citrus* species. Some species have glands throughout the leaf, while in others they are restricted to the leaf margins. Hold a makrut lime leaf up to the light and you'll see hundreds of glands, visible as translucent dots all over the surface.

Looking at a makrut lime leaf, it doesn't take long to notice that it has an unusual shape. The blade representing the distal (upper) part of the leaf appears conjoined with a secondary blade below it. And this curious character is only one of the various leaf forms found within the rue family. Some species display so-called trifoliolate leaves, the leaf blades comprising three separate leaflets (e.g. *Poncirus trifoliata*), while others have palmately compound leaves with up to five leaflets (e.g. *Casimiroa*). In some cases the leaves are pinnately compound, as in prickly ash (see page 189), or even bipinnate, with two sets of leaflets, as in members of the genus *Ruta*, for which the family is named. *Citrus* is known to have descended from compound-leaved ancestors. As such, single-bladed *Citrus* leaves are the result of an evolutionary reduction in the number of leaf parts, and the leaves are unifoliolate; that is, compound, but consisting of a single leaflet. A small joint or slight swelling indicates where the leaflet stem joins the end of the petiole. The *Citrus* petiole is often endowed with flanges of tissue to either side of the petiole. Known, not surprisingly, as wings, they are particularly apparent in makrut lime, to the extent that the flanges are expanded and leaf-like, and sometimes even as large as the blade to which they are attached.

Notably too, the leaves of most cultivated *Citrus* taxa are often conduplicate, or folded up lengthwise. This is a mechanism that many trees employ to reduce water loss by limiting the potential for evapotranspiration in response to excessive heat. Thus, *Citrus* leaves usually sit flat when subjected to shade but are sharply folded up when exposed to full sunshine. The difference in leaf angle between leaves on the outside of a crown compared with those on the inside can be marked.

Citrus species are not alone in having wonderfully winged petioles. This character is also found in members of the trumpet creeper family (Bignoniaceae), though evidently never in the catalpas (see Indian bean tree, page 277).

The variable, and sometimes curious, leaf morphology of *Citrus* plants is a result of the genus's propensity for mutation, though the results are more readily observed in the huge variety of fruits they have spawned. While makrut lime is a species in its own right, several other cultivated citruses have more convoluted histories. Those widely grown today derive from perhaps a handful of ancestral species that have given rise to numerous selections and hybrids, both ancient and recent. In some cases, as with the cultivated lemons, their origins are virtually untraceable. Grapefruit, on the other hand, is only around 300 years old, being a human discovery of an accidental hybrid. The selection of novel *Citrus* fruits is indeed rather a common occurrence, with this reflected on supermarket shelves. *Citrus* trees themselves are also increasingly offered and are a not-so-infrequent sight in greenhouses, as well as outdoors in regions that are mostly frost-free. Their value for both foliage and fruit renders *Citrus* trees a popular choice for kitchen gardeners across the world.

FORMIDABLE DEFENCES

Plants, in a state of nature, are always warring with
one another, contending for the monopoly of the soil,
the stronger ejecting the weaker, the more vigorous
overgrowing and killing the more delicate. Every
modification of climate, every disturbance of the soil,
every interference with the existing vegetation of an
area, favours some species at the expense of others.

JOSEPH DALTON HOOKER

*People are often surprised at the degree to which plants have
evolved to protect themselves. But one needs only look at the vora-
ciousness of people to understand the evolutionary pressures for
defence. If we can eat or use them otherwise, a plant's leaves are
stripped away. In established cultures people soon learn to
moderate their harvests, but animals have no such compunction.
When monkey puzzle trees first arose, 200 million years ago, the
attending herbivores were gigantic Triassic dinosaurs. Chances
are, if their leaves weren't as tough as old boots the trees wouldn't
be here today. Varnish tree, too, is not something to be trifled with,
but not for want of armature; its defences are entirely internal.
Alluadia and prickly ash, like varnish tree, are much more recent
introductions, geologically speaking, but the leaves of the prickly
species are no less inviting to herbivores. Their protective strategies
are somewhat more conventional, but still effective. It's interesting
to speculate on the pressures that brought about more intimidating
leaf-borne defences in flowering plants – such as those in the
Australian gympie gympie trees. Read on!*

GIANT
STINGING
TREE

Dendrocnide excelsa

Australia is well known for being home to some of the world's most dangerous animals. Snakes, spiders and snails are only some of the highly venomous animals native to the country, not to mention the dangers of crocodiles; even male magpies that swoop in spring should not be taken lightly. But Australia is home to some of the most dangerous plant species on the planet, too, none more so than those in the genus *Dendrocnide*, the so-called 'stinging trees' (which translates almost directly). Six species occur in subtropical and tropical parts of eastern Australia, their potent, pain-inducing properties equal to, or even greater than, those of the more mobile venom producers.

Stinging trees belong to the nettle family, Urticaceae, which has a nearly global distribution, and as well as trees and shrubs contains several herbs, including the common stinging nettle (*Urtica dioica*). The nettle's use as a tonic is as well known as its sting, though its historic use – inducing inflammation as a treatment for arthritis – seems somewhat dubious, at best.

There are 37 recognised species in *Dendrocnide*, distributed across parts of Southeast Asia, India, the Pacific Islands and Australia. The genus contains shrubs as well as trees, with *D. excelsa* endemic to Australia and growing to heights of more than 40 metres. It is fittingly known as the giant stinging tree, and is also called Australian nettle tree or fibrewood. Its ample leaves are broad and heart-shaped, with toothed margins. The leaves, stems and fruits are covered with short, hair-like structures known as trichomes; these are the source of the sting for which *Dendrocnide* is named. Indeed, all stinging members of the nettle family have them.

Though not particularly potent in the common stinging nettle, in the giant stinging tree the sting is a serious matter. While the trichomes might look soft and inviting to touch, they are in fact anything but. A minor sting lasts for an hour or so, and severe stings can cause pain for months. Stinging occurs as the tips of the trichomes – which are strengthened with silica – break off and penetrate the skin, acting like a miniature hypodermic needle. The trichomes inject toxins that cause major allergic reactions, which include intense burning, swelling and even debilitating, morphine-resistant pain. Those working in forests where the species occurs often go in armed with heavy-duty gloves, masks and antihistamines, though without guarantee that these will suffice if the worst happens.

And as if the sting of the giant stinging tree wasn't bad enough, that of the fellow eastern Australian *Dendrocnide moroides* – known by its Aboriginal name gympie gympie – is even worse. The slightest touch results in unbearable pain, and a bad sting can result in severe swelling and throbbing in the lymph nodes under the arms, which can last several hours. Stinging trees can also cause sneezing, nosebleeds and significant respiratory damage from merely staying too close to them for longer than around twenty minutes without adequate protection. Sting victims have been known to require hospital visits and intensive care. Among its many alternative common names is 'suicide plant', due to stories of people not being able to endure the pain caused by an altercation with the gympie gympie.

The mechanics of the pain caused by *Dendrocnide* stings are not well understood, but recently researchers isolated a previously uncharacterised group of neurotoxins from both the giant stinging tree and the gympie gympie shrub. These compounds have been termed 'gympietides' and are thought to be the root cause of the long-term pain that stinging trees inflict. In a remarkable instance of convergent evolution, gympietides have a chemical structure similar to toxins found in the venom of both spiders and scorpions. Equally incredibly, the leaves of stinging trees retain their toxicity for decades. Even 100-year-old, dried botanical specimens can sting.

Recommended treatment for *Dendrocnide* stings has generally been to apply diluted hydrochloric acid to the wound to nullify the trichome's protective coating, then to use hair-waxing strips to remove the trichomes themselves. This would, in theory, bring relief within a couple of hours. If not removed, hairs can remain in the skin for six months, causing pain whenever irritated by touch or water. However, it is thought that the long-term pain caused by a *Dendrocnide* sting may not be because of hairs becoming lodged in the skin, but rather a result of the injected gympietides both generating pain signals and suppressing mechanisms in the body that stop these signals. On a positive note, this new insight may help in our understanding of how stings can be better treated and inform the development of new painkillers.

Despite their toxicity to humans, *Dendrocnide* leaves are eaten by numerous insects, birds and marsupials, including by the wallaby-like red-legged pademelon. Stinging tree fruit is also considered edible once the hairs are removed, though its preparation seems something of a high-risk activity that is arguably not worth the trouble, especially as they are reputed not to have much taste. There is also anecdotal evidence that some *Dendrocnide* plants don't sting at all, but who would want to check that?

VARNISH TREE

Toxicodendron vernicifluum

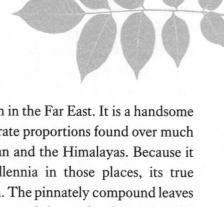

Varnish tree is well known in the Far East. It is a handsome deciduous tree of moderate proportions found over much of China, and in Korea, Japan and the Himalayas. Because it has been cultivated for millennia in those places, its true nativity may never be known. The pinnately compound leaves and stout twigs are reminiscent of those of walnuts, but the crown of the varnish tree is more generously endowed with branches, and the leaves more numerous and densely clustered toward the branch tips. They are yellow-green and softly hairy when expanding. Each leaf stalk ascends stiffly at a sharp angle, and has a drooping tip that gradually straightens out as the stalk lengthens and matures toward a more horizontal posture. When expanding, the leaflets are conspicuously corrugated, with rows of impressed veins on either side of the midrib. These wrinkles gradually stretch and the leaflets become surprisingly papery and smooth, though a scrim of downy hairs is usually retained on the undersides.

Compared with other temperate pinnate-leaved trees, varnish trees look particularly lush, with individual leaflets that are mostly uniform and tightly spaced. Flowers are produced in summer, and trees can be strictly male or female, or polygamous (consisting of both male and female flowers). Although tiny, the flowers are borne in ample, yellow-green panicles that briefly stand in loose pyramids above the opulent foliage, drooping as they age. By the time the yellow pea-sized drupes are ripe in autumn, the panicles are fully pendent. Autumn leaf colour in varnish trees is variable – some trees fleetingly blaze orange or red, but mostly the leaflets merely fade to pale yellow-green before they fall.

As attractive as these trees are, they are less known as ornamentals than as trees of cultural importance. It's what's inside that gives this species its considerable notoriety. The latex derived from *T. vernicifluum* is the traditional source of lacquer used for coating wooden screens, trays, tables and boxes in China, Korea and Japan. The earliest known use of lacquer dates from more than 9,000 years ago in Japan, but lacquerware is still produced across Southeast Asia. Multiple applications of lacquer provide a surface onto which any decoration or inlay is applied, with a smooth, hard, high-gloss, waterproof shell. Oriental lacquerware pieces are often highly valued, not only due to the exquisite finish, but because the expense of the lacquer itself makes it worthy of only the most valuable *objets d'art*. The tapping of varnish trees to obtain the latex is a slow and painstaking procedure, and potentially dangerous as well.

Toxicodendron is a member of the family Anacardiaceae, which is well known both for food plants – including cashews, pistachios and mangoes – and also interesting, often hazardous, chemistry. Some common ornamental anacards – such as smoke tree (*Cotinus coggygria*) and staghorn sumac (*Rhus typhina*) – have caustic sap, and many have been used in folk medicine. For example, a tea to treat gastric problems is made from the bark of chuachalalate (*Amphipterygium adstringens*), a rare Mexican relative of the cashew (*Anacadium occidentale*). Another, the Peruvian pepper tree (*Schinus molle*), which is a noxious weed in subtropical regions around the world and the source of pink peppercorns, is being investigated for its insecticidal properties.

With a name like *Toxicodendron*, which means 'poison tree', it shouldn't be surprising that there are serious risks attributed to it. *Toxicodendron* species were originally recognised as being part of *Rhus* (sumac), but were hived off to their own primarily on account of their production of urushiol, an oily compound that causes serious contact dermatitis in approximately three-quarters of those who encounter it. Poison ivy (*T. radicans*) is familiar to and assiduously avoided by most North Americans for the same reason. All parts of the varnish tree are similarly endowed with urushiol – appropriately, the name *vernicifluum* means 'flowing with varnish'.

So, how can an exudate so noxious produce a compound so fine and useful? In Southeast Asia, where varnish tree is native, high humidity and warm temperatures provide ideal conditions to change the oily, urushiol-containing latex into high-quality lacquer. Varnish tappers are lucky if they can avoid touching the toxic latex, but even touching the bark, stems or leaves of *T. vernicifluum* can cause a serious allergic reaction. Urushiol is particularly insidious in its ability to both persist on surfaces and be quickly absorbed through the skin. This is why the species, once common in botanical collections, and much celebrated both for its beauty and utility, is now rarely planted.

MADAGASCAR OCOTILLO

Alluaudia procera

In a contest for the planet's strangest tree, Madagascar ocotillo would definitely be in the running. The species is the largest and most arborescent of the alluaudias, members of the equally weird octopus-tree family, Didiereaceae. For years, botanists were unsure where to place these spiny, xerophytic shrubs and trees endemic to (found only in) Madagascar's spiny forest ecoregion.

Madagascar ocotillo begins life very un-tree-like. It generally forms a tangled thicket of looping branches close to the ground, building up its reserves until, eventually, plants can produce stems of sufficient diameter to hold themselves vertical. These invigorated stems ultimately produce stout, similarly ascending, but sinuous branches. Trees, yes, but they look like they might have been made up by Dr Seuss.

Southern Madagascar is hot year-round, with a long, dry season and sparse winter rainfall, and in the spiny forest ecoregion the soils are not particularly rich. Despite these ecological hardships, endemism is high, and the area has been recognised for its unique biodiversity. Plants in desert climates like this one often survive by retaining water in succulent tissues or by shedding leaves and becoming dormant until moisture returns. Alluaudias have adopted both adaptations to survive under these difficult conditions. Madagascar ocotillo has succulent stems and deciduous, succulent leaves – features shared with a number of other spiny plants, including its south-west North American name-sake, the ocotillo (*Fouquieria splendens*). As similar as these two appear, they are only distantly related; the resemblance to the North American ocotillo is a trick of convergent evolution. Convergence describes features that are adaptive in one environment (like wings that allow hovering, fins that facilitate swimming, or spiny stems that prevent predation), and that evolve independently in similar environments. This phenomenon is more common than might be realised – think hummingbirds and hawkmoths (a hovering bird and a hovering insect), or sharks and dolphins (a finned fish and a finned mammal). The two ocotillos are readily differentiated when flowering. *Fouquieria* has showy, red, hummingbird-pollinated flowers, while in the Madagascar ocotillo, the flowers are produced in loose, thin, pompom-like clusters at the tip of the branches.

Both the stems and leaves of the Madagascar ocotillo are succulent. Like other succulent plants, they utilise a particular physiology that differs from that of non-succulents. In photosynthesis, carbon dioxide is absorbed through open leaf stomata (the pores for gas exchange). At the same time, water vapour from inside the leaf is lost to the atmosphere. It is the difference between the amount of water vapour inside the leaf and that outside, which is the engine that draws moisture up from the roots, through the stems and leaves and away from the leaf. This is the transpiration stream, and the loss from plants is known as evapotranspiration. In a desert climate the difference between the atmospheric humidity and the humidity inside the leaf can be enormous. Thus, the opening of stomata on a hot day can be a serious liability, particularly if water is in short supply. To counter the loss, succulent plants employ crassulacean acid metabolism, which allows a version of photosynthesis to take place at night (see *Dioon*, page 13).

An adaptation employed by the Madagascar ocotillo that helps keep leaves cool is their vertical or near-vertical alignment, such that the full force of the sun's rays is intercepted not by their broad surfaces, but by their margins. A less obvious adaptation is the nearly round shape and small size of the leaf and the lack of a petiole (leaf stem). These features create a near optimal radiative surface; that is, a surface that effectively dissipates rather than accumulates heat. The best radiators are characterised by a small surface area relative to a large edge (think of the length of the fins on a car radiator). But note that the car radiator relies on high wind velocity for cooling. With leaves, the smaller and rounder, the greater is the edge-to-surface ratio. More importantly, the smaller the leaf, the less air flow is required to draw away heat. So, Madagascar ocotillo is clearly supremely adapted to its environment; but we've neglected an important issue common to plants everywhere, which is to say: who's having the leaves for lunch?

The spines of the Madagascar ocotillo, like the arma-
ments of other desert plants, provide a modicum of shade
to the stems – and, if the plant has them, to the leaves
– but importantly, spines are an adaptation that keeps
herbivores at bay. Spines are actually modified leaves.
Anatomically, they are little different from normal leaves
when first forming, but they don't develop the ability to
photosynthesise and they eventually become hardened,
sharp-pointed and more or less permanent. In dry, desert
climates, herbivores are relentless in their appetite for nutri-
ent- and moisture-rich leaves. In the case of Madagascar
ocotillo, the most common herbivore is the omnivorous
(and very charismatic) ring-tailed lemur (*Lemur catta*).
The leaves are highly sought after by them, but standing
in their way are rows of formidable, close-set spines that
line the silvery stems. Unfortunately for the lemur, the
succulent leaves are wedged in between an upper and a
lower spine, with each leaf barely sticking out past impressive batteries of them. In this battle, the tree is the clear
winner. The ring-tailed lemur is only able to feed in a
limited way because of the defensive placement of the
formidable spines. Nevertheless, there is evidence that
an extinct giant primate, a baboon- or even gorilla-sized
lemur (*Hadropithecus stenognathus*) was native to the same
area, and, according to paleontological studies of their skull
shape, mandibles and teeth, it appears that *Hadropithecus*
would have been more than a match for the spiny stems,
and probably fed on its leaves. The giant lemur is known
to have become extinct sometime before the eighth century
CE, soon after humans arrived in Madagascar. Sadly, both
the ring-tailed lemur and the Madagascar ocotillo are now

threatened by deforestation, and extinction is a definite possibility. A mere 2,000 lemurs are now known in the wild, their declining numbers mostly due to habitat destruction, hunting and the exotic pet trade.

PRICKLY ASH

Zanthoxylum ailanthoides

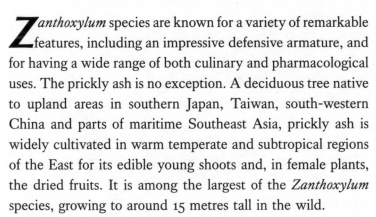

*Z*anthoxylum species are known for a variety of remarkable features, including an impressive defensive armature, and for having a wide range of both culinary and pharmacological uses. The prickly ash is no exception. A deciduous tree native to upland areas in southern Japan, Taiwan, south-western China and parts of maritime Southeast Asia, prickly ash is widely cultivated in warm temperate and subtropical regions of the East for its edible young shoots and, in female plants, the dried fruits. It is among the largest of the *Zanthoxylum* species, growing to around 15 metres tall in the wild.

The most striking characteristic of the prickly ash is the serious nature of its defences. Medium to large, sparsely branched trees with large, pinnately compound leaves, the prickly ash has stems, leaf stalks and leaf-backs abundantly armed with prickles. The lower branches display large, prickle-tipped knobs that give the bark a wildly uneven texture. Further up the stems and stalks, the prickles are more like those of roses or brambles. On the undersides of the leaves they are smaller, but are still considerable impediments to handling. In all cases, *Zanthoxylum* prickles have a broad base and very sharp, recurved tip; these are effective at reducing the activities of grazing animals.

Plants furnished with protective armature are generally referred to as spinescent, whether or not the plant bears actual spines. Any sharpened feature will do. The common holly (*Ilex aquifolium*) has spinose leaf margins, the may (*Crataegus monogyna*) thorny branches and the Himalayan blackberry (*Rubus bifrons*) is savagely prickly. All are considered spinescent. True spines are modified leaves, and thorns modified branches. Regardless of what anyone says about roses, the sharp bits are prickles, not thorns, as in the prickly ash.

Technically, prickles are modifications of the epidermis. They begin as trichomes (hair-like structures) on the plant's surface, and somehow grow larger than the hairs around them. The mechanisms that cause the hairs to develop further into a prickle are not well understood, but, crucially, prickles have no connection with the plant's vasculature. In contrast, spines and thorns have vascular bundles and are connected to the plant's internal water-works. As a prickle ages, its cells become lignified, but without an internal source of water they cannot continue to divide, so they quickly die. On a woody stem like a rose, the expansion of the stem under the prickle causes the prickle base to eventually lose its connection with the bark and detach. But while a hardened prickle cannot expand, on the stems of *Zanthoxylum* the corky bark around the prickle's base continues to grow as though it were a vascularised branch, and it carries the prickle outward with the thickening bark. This results in older prickly ash branches being studded with often huge conical, prickle-tipped 'bark emergences'.

Prickly ash leaves are exceptionally lush. They are pinnately compound, composed of up to 23 narrow leaflets, arranged in two opposite ranks along a grooved rachis. In the sun, the leaflets often fold upwards along the midrib, and the long tips curve to the side. The leaves can be nearly a metre long, and the individual leaflets 15 centimetres or more in length, the size of leaves and leaflets increasing with the vigour of the shoot and the amount of shade. The ample leaves are somewhat reminiscent of those of tree of heaven (*Ailanthus altissima*), hence the epithet *ailanthoides*, which means '*Ailanthus*-like'. When held up to the light, translucent dots can be seen scattered regularly across the leaflet surface. The structures, which are known as pellucid dots, are secretory oil glands and give the plants their distinctive spicy aroma. These are a common feature throughout the citrus family (see Makrut lime, page 167) Rutaceae, to which *Zanthoxylum* also belongs.

While the armature of the prickly ash leaves is essentially like those of brambles or roses – that is, smallish prickles restricted to the petiole and rachis on the underside of the leaf – the density and size of prickles is variable. Some individual trees are exceptionally well-endowed, while others are barely armed at all. Research undertaken on a few small islands in southern Japan has shown that prickle size on prickly ash leaves is correlated with browse pressure from native deer. The studies show that the greater the density of deer on the island, the fiercer the prickles displayed, and that completely unarmed plants are known to inhabit historically deer-free islands.

All parts of the prickly ash produce a potent mixture of

aromatic chemicals, and these are also thought to deter predators. However, as deer are known to feed on the leaves whether they have prickles or not, the chemistry is more likely there to discourage insect pests and fight off fungal attacks. Indeed, numerous compounds have been identified in a wide range of *Zanthoxylum* species that have effective insecticidal and antimicrobial properties. Nevertheless, the caterpillars of several kinds of Asian swallowtail butterflies (*Papilio* species) feed on the leaves of the prickly ash. Swallowtail butterflies are well known for their ability to safely ingest otherwise toxic compounds from *Zanthoxylum*, *Citrus* and other rutaceous plants. These compounds in turn provide defensive chemicals for the caterpillars and butterflies.

In Asia, the leaves, bark and root bark have been used in traditional medicine for centuries. Their uses include treatments for the common cold, bruising, snakebite and circulatory issues. The strong, peppery flavour of the fruits and leaves of this and several other *Zanthoxylum* species lend the characteristic piquancy to regional East Asian cuisines (e.g. Sichuan cooking). The tiny fruits of a number of Asian species are known as Sichuan pepper. Prior to the introduction to Asia in the late fifteenth century of chili peppers (*Capsicum* species) – so ubiquitous in Asian cooking that they are often thought of as traditional, but are in fact native to Mexico – the only 'hot' spices there were *Zanthoxylum* species, black pepper (*Piper nigrum*) and ginger (*Zingiber officinale*).

In China and Taiwan young prickly ash leaves are eaten raw or, more commonly, cooked to garnish meat and fish dishes. They are also sometimes battered and deep-fried. In Taiwan, an aboriginal group known as the Tayal have a legend that a hunter who was nearly lost in the mountains with only some nearly spoiled, salted pork to eat happened across prickly ash, which was so pleasingly aromatic that he used the leaves to improve the flavour of the meat. Impressed with his discovery and wanting to share it with his people, the hunter brought it home, where it became a traditional element of their cuisine.

When chewed, the leaves and fruits have a surprisingly intense, tingling-numbing effect in the mouth – hence the alternate common name, toothache tree. The compound involved, alkylamide hydroxy-α-sanshool – found in all *Zanthoxylum* species – has been proven in clinical trials to effectively reduce both sharp, acute pain and inflammatory pain, and so it is being tested as an analgesic (painkiller) and in the treatment of rheumatoid arthritis.

Prickly ash is also an impressive ornamental tree. With so many exceptional features, it's hard to know why it is not better known. If you see one in the flesh, take a moment to savour its pungent aromas and consider its potential.

MONKEY PUZZLE

Araucaria araucana

The monkey puzzle tree is perhaps the most easily recognised of all conifers. In youth, its crown habit is pyramidal; it becomes more cone-like with age, though always retains a seemingly impossible symmetrical form. Thick, lateral branches are produced in regular whorls of five up the stem, each clothed with overlapping, broad yet stout, scale-like leathery leaves with wickedly pointed tips. These are dark green, with white bands of stomata visible on both surfaces.

One of the most striking things about monkey puzzle leaves is their arrangement. Densely set and spiralling all the way around the branches, this distinctive phyllotaxy points to its need for maximum sun exposure to all parts of the crown. Spiral phyllotaxy is in fact quite frequent among trees – exhibited by some oaks (*Quercus*) and sweet gums (*Liquidambar*), for example – though here less markedly so, given the larger gaps between leaves along branches. Ultimately, it is always about achieving optimal exposure to the sun.

The leaves of the monkey puzzle, however, have another distinctive characteristic that is frequently seen throughout the plant world: their leaves are arranged in the Fibonacci sequence. Named after the thirteenth-century Italian mathematician, also known as Leonardo da Pisa, the Fibonacci sequence is a mathematical progression. Each number in the sequence follows the rule that the next number is the sum of the previous two, hence '0', '1', then '1', '2', '3', '5', '8', '13', '21', '34', and so on. In plants, the sequence is readily recognised in the patterns of disc florets, or the 'face', of the common sunflower (*Helianthus annuus*), or other species belonging to the daisy family, Asteraceae. These have multiple sets of florets spiralling from the centre outwards, one set clockwise, the other anticlockwise. Counting the number of spirals, each reveals them to be adjacent numbers in the Fibonacci sequence (typically, 34 in one direction and 55 in the other).

To count spirals of (sharp!) monkey puzzle leaves is a painstaking business, best undertaken with gloves. It is considerably easier to view the spirals on the trunk and older branches, where the normal expansion of the shoot separates the leaves and more clearly exposes the pattern. The Fibonacci sequence shows up in the monkey puzzle's seed-cones and in other conifer cones as well. Curious, perhaps, yet an exceedingly common pattern in all sorts of plants, not merely sunflowers and conifers. The rosette leaves of succulents, red-hot poker (*Kniphofia*) flowers and pineapples all exhibit Fibonacci spirals. And it doesn't stop there. The sequence comes up again and again because these particular spirals describe the most efficient packing patterns in nature – and the more you look for them, the more of them you will see.

Monkey puzzles are among the (vast majority of) conifers that are evergreen, with crowns always clothed with leaves. Being an evergreen doesn't mean that a tree retains its leaves for ever; rather that they are continually replaced and the tree never has a truly leafless phase. There are several modes of evergreen habit. Some trees are termed 'leaf exchangers', where leaves persist for less than a year, but are replaced so that there are always functioning leaves in the crown. 'Semi-evergreen' trees drop their old leaves immediately after fresh ones emerge, while 'semi-deciduous' trees lose more than half their leaves, but are never completely bare.

Monkey puzzles, though, are emphatically evergreen. Their leaves are in fact amazingly persistent, typically remaining functionally photosynthetic for 10 to 15 years and, in exceptional cases, up to 25 or even 30 years. The bristlecone pine (*Pinus longaeva*) is capable of retaining its leaves for a similar length of time, though most fully evergreen trees replace their leaves far more frequently, with cycles of every three to five years, or up to every ten years in firs (*Abies*) and spruces (*Picea*), the most common strategy.

Old monkey puzzle leaves often remain embedded in the grey-brown resinous bark of the trunk for decades before wearing away or being completely engulfed. And when it comes to shedding, sometimes, instead of dropping individual leaves, trees will shed entire branches, particularly those from the lower reaches of its stem. Thus, after a few hundred years, a tree will develop a broad, umbrella-shaped crown.

The species is native to parts of Chile and Argentina, its distribution straddling both sides of the southern Andes at elevations between 600 and 1,800 metres in areas of high rain and snowfall on loose volcanic soils. It is thus adapted to disturbance, and has thick bark that protects it from wildfires. Unusually for a conifer, monkey puzzles can regenerate themselves from dormant buds in response to serious injury (or felling). Unfortunately, the trees are threatened in the wild due to a combination of increased fire, logging and overgrazing.

Both the genus name and specific epithet refer to the Spanish word '*Araucana*', for both the Mapuche indigenous people and the region where this species is found. The monkey puzzle was an important tree in Mapuche culture, not least for its huge, starch-rich edible seeds. Boiled or roasted, they taste like chestnuts (*Castanea*) and are still eaten by locals nowadays.

A common and often arresting sight, monkey puzzles have been in cultivation in the West since the end of the eighteenth century, when Archibald Menzies, the surgeon-botanist accompanying Captain Vancouver on HMS *Discovery*, who was attending a banquet with the Governor of Chile, apparently pocketed a handful of seeds that were supposed to be for his dessert. He successfully grew plants on the way home, which he then presented to Sir Joseph Banks, then advisor to King George III on the development of the Royal Botanic Gardens, Kew, who planted specimens at his private residence in London. At this point, no one was referring to the trees as 'monkey puzzles'. It was more than 50 years later that a visitor to a Cornish garden opined that 'it would puzzle a monkey to climb that'. The moniker 'monkey puzzler' was adopted first, before the 'r' was later dropped. It is of course the sharp, forward-pointing leaves that are problematic to any potential climber, and while it may be possible for a monkey to climb *up* the tree, navigating the trunk and branches is presumed possible in only this direction. Sadly, there are no monkeys native to this part of South America with which to test the theory.

The monkey puzzle family occurs largely in the Southern Hemisphere but was once far more widespread. Araucaria fossils have been found dating back to the late Triassic Period, nearly 200 million years ago, while the genus is thought to have been nearly worldwide in tropical regions through the remainder of the Mesozoic Era (approximately 252 to 66 million years ago). They became extinct in the Northern Hemisphere after this time, and had become increasingly limited to their present distribution by the Tertiary Period (approximately 66 million to 2.6 million years ago). The gemstone known as jet, used as jewellery in Europe by Romans and Vikings, as well as by Queen Victoria as part of her mourning attire, is derived from the wood of trees of the monkey puzzle family. It is a product of the wood's degradation following waterlogging, burial, compaction and heating over millions of years.

As well as the distinctive monkey puzzle, the *Araucaria* genus also includes the Norfolk Island Pine (*A. heterophylla*), a similarly common component of Mediterranean landscapes and a popular houseplant in temperate regions. However, as its name suggests, it is native to Norfolk Island, in the South Pacific. The Tropical South Pacific is a centre of diversity for *Araucaria* species, with 14 of the 20 species found on the cluster of islands that make up New Caledonia. This territory is renowned for its broader coniferous diversity, with around 43 species occurring there, all of them endemic.

The monkey puzzle family also contains the Kauri pine (*Agathis australis*) of New Zealand, and the Australian Wollemi pine (*Wollemia nobilis*), the discovery of which in 1994 took the botanical world by storm, with cultivated specimens fast becoming a 'must-have' tree among the dendrological community. A specimen at Kew Gardens, London, was kept in a cage for several years, drawing attention to its presence there and its restricted wild occurrence in gorges in Wollemi National Park, New South Wales. The only wild plants were narrowly saved from eradication by bush fires in 2019.

Around a third of the world's conifer species are threatened with extinction in the wild. In the monkey puzzle family, a staggering two-thirds are at risk. While monkey puzzles are known to be good at holding on to their leaves, how good are we at holding on to the trees themselves?

EXTRAORDINARY ATTRIBUTES

I never saw a discontented tree. They grip the
ground as though they liked it, and though fast
rooted they travel about as far as we do.

JOHN MUIR

*Countless plants can be set apart by virtue of their size, age or
beauty. The more familiar these special plants, the less extraordinary any one might seem, but there are a few that really
do make an impression, standing above the fray. Size is an
obvious yardstick on which to measure greatness. In terms of
leaves, Brazilian fern tree, bigleaf magnolia and giant seagrape
are all stupendous, and each is exceptional in other ways, as
well. Paleontology also figures in these accounts. Dawn redwood,
Tasmanian tree fern and ginkgo (old, older, oldest) possess
different ancient features, as can be seen in the fossil record, and
each is fascinating in its own right. Catalina ironwood is also
renowned for its (much younger) geological history, but mostly
for its arresting foliar beauty. The leaves of the sacred fig and the
tree itself are also celebrated.*

CATALINA IRONWOOD

Lyonothamnus floribundus

The Channel Islands off the south coast of California have a history replete with the forces of geological change, momentous human firsts and almost unbelievable tales of exotic animals, but there are fascinating plants there, too. While we are familiar with climate change and the prospect of dramatically rising sea levels, during the Pleistocene Glaciation (the most recent Ice Age), sea levels across the world were as much as 120 metres lower than they are today. This in part allowed migrations of people across the Bering Land Bridge into North America. For the Channel Islands it meant that the gap between the archipelago and the mainland coast was narrower than it is today and that the smaller clusters of islands formed larger mega-islands. This would have facilitated prehistoric exchange of both plants and animals.

Though perhaps difficult to imagine, bison-sized pygmy mammoths (*Mammuthus exilis*) were common in the Channel Islands. These pachyderms were descendants of the more widespread Columbia mammoth (*Mammuthus columbi*). More amazing still, the earliest paleontological evidence of humans in North America is from remains discovered in the Channel Islands dated at 13,000 years ago, a mere blink before pygmy mammoths became extinct there.

Prior to the Pleistocene Epoch (approximately 2.6 million to 12,000 years ago), the progenitor of Catalina ironwood was distributed more widely across south-western North America, but as the climate shifted and became drier, the species died out, stranding remaining populations in the Channel Islands. Several other plants and animals shared a similar, if somewhat less orphan-like, fate. The island Torrey pine (*Pinus torreyana* var. *insularis*), island tree mallow (*Malva assurgentiflora*), island fence lizard (*Sceloporus occidentalis beckii*) and cat-sized island fox (*Urocyron littoralis*) are some of the more charismatic examples of Channel Island endemics; however, they are all descended from more widespread species that still exist on the mainland. Because Catalina ironwood's closest relatives are extinct, the species is considered a 'relictual endemic'.

Catalina ironwood is a small tree with shredding bark and evergreen leaves, mostly found in canyons, on rocky slopes and in oak woodlands, where it grows 5 to 15 metres tall. The wood is very hard and the bark can be striking, peeling in long shreds and exposing rust-streaked, smoother grey bark beneath. Unusual for a member of the rose family (Rosaceae), the leaves are arranged in opposite pairs on the stems. Still, the small flowers are fairly typical of the family, with five whitish petals and five green sepals. The individual flowers are crowded into broad heads that sit above the foliage in spring.

In most Catalina ironwood groves the stems are derived from the same genetically distinct individuals. In other words, the groves are clonal stands. This suggested to early conservation biologists that there was a problem with normal reproduction by seed. It was observed with cultivated Catalina ironwood, however, that plants are indeed capable of producing viable seed and normal seedlings. They also noted that the stems of seedlings are naturally weak, which makes them particularly susceptible to both trampling and browsing by animals. Unfortunately, feral animals were and still are very common across the Islands.

At first blush, there appear to be two distinctive forms of this Channel Islands species. The most widespread manifestation, and the one usually seen in cultivation, has large, wide-spreading compound leaves. This entity is often dubbed subspecies *aspleniifolius*. A rarer form – sometimes known as subspecies *floribundus* – is characterised by leaves that are simple and lance-shaped. One would be hard-pressed to consider them the same species, but botanists point out that there is considerable variation in leaf shape within the populations and genetic similarity among plants across the range. Although people have selected plants from among the populations that show marked differences, the populations actually show a range of leaf variation, and there is no convenient biological marker to set the two apart. Despite this, many follow a less rigid view and recognise two separate subspecies.

The largest, most elaborate leaves of Catalina ironwood are exceptionally attractive. They are usually constructed with a long, central leaflet terminating in an equally long petiole, and between two and six spreading leaflets that diverge in pairs from lower on the central axis. Each leaflet is lance-shaped in outline, but intriguingly segmented, with more than a dozen densely stacked, wing-shaped lobes. The shape is so unusual that one might be forgiven for thinking it unique, but it is not. A number of other plants have arrived at this particular leaf design, including the remarkably similar-looking sweet fern (*Comptonia peregrina*), which isn't a fern, and a number of true ferns, such as the maidenhair spleenwort (*Asplenium trichomanes*), from which this variant gets its name (*aspleni* = spleenwort + *folium* = leaf).

Catalina is the Channel Island from which *Lyonothamnus floribundus* gets its common name. It is the island closest to Los Angeles (only 42 kilometres away) and the only one to have significant permanent civilian settlements. (There are military installations on other islands, but no resort hotels or extensive neighbourhoods as there are on Catalina.) The island, which is also known as Santa Catalina, was once a popular escape for the rich and famous, being so easily accessed from Los Angeles by private boat or ferry. Famously, a herd of 14 American bison was transported to the island in 1924 for the production of a silent Western movie, *The Thundering Herd*. They were left to fend for themselves after the movie wrapped and, in the absence of predators, the herd eventually grew to more than 500 individuals. After judicious culling, the remainder – around 150 – now roam freely on the island. They are an appealing, if somewhat startling spectacle for the million or so annual visitors, and have become unofficial mascots for the island. Catalina ironwood is threatened by all manner of exotic grazers and browsers, but nearly all have been effectively eradicated on the island of Catalina.

Only mule deer and bison remain there, and while the deer's days may be numbered, the enduring popularity of the bison suggests that Catalina ironwood might always have to put up with some level of bovine nibbling.

BIGLEAF
MAGNOLIA

Magnolia macrophylla

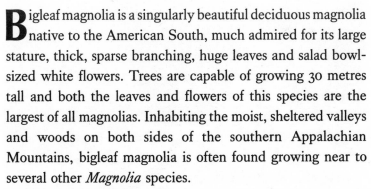

Bigleaf magnolia is a singularly beautiful deciduous magnolia native to the American South, much admired for its large stature, thick, sparse branching, huge leaves and salad bowl-sized white flowers. Trees are capable of growing 30 metres tall and both the leaves and flowers of this species are the largest of all magnolias. Inhabiting the moist, sheltered valleys and woods on both sides of the southern Appalachian Mountains, bigleaf magnolia is often found growing near to several other *Magnolia* species.

The first European to catalogue the species was the French botanist and explorer André Michaux, in 1759. He subsequently exported the species to Europe, where it caused a sensation among the gardening cognoscenti. The broader eastern United States is recognised as a region of considerable biodiversity, home to eight different *Magnolia* species. Across the world, there are some 300 species, most of them subtropical and tropical trees inhabiting Southeast Asia and Central and South America, but there are a few cold-hardy ones, and many of these, including bigleaf magnolia, are grown in gardens. Cold-tolerant magnolias hail only from east Asia and eastern North America – one species even makes it as far north as south-eastern Canada. The conditions that are common to all of these areas – tropical to temperate – is near constant moisture and soils that are rich and usually well drained.

Magnolias are considered among the more primitive of the flowering plants. They show up in the fossil record around ninety-five million years ago. The waterlilies and some other small aquatic plants are older, but magnolias retain a number of 'primitive' features and are frequently associated with imagined prehistoric landscapes as one might see in the movies. Plants in the magnolia family, Magnoliaceae, produce a variety of aromatic compounds in their tissues, and these are mainly feeding deterrents. Considering how long they've been around, it's a good question what sort of animals these chemicals evolved to deter. The potent cocktail of chemicals in magnolia is often expressed to the greatest degree in the bark. The Cherokee tribe traditionally used the bark as an analgesic, a gastrointestinal and respiratory aid, and a tooth-ache remedy.

Magnolias are frequently grown for their flowers, and these are white or in rare instances pink or purple, and sweetly scented, with parts that are arranged spirally (a common feature of primitive flowering plants) around a stout axis. There are no separate petals and sepals, as one might see with a rose or hibiscus flower, but a set of undifferentiated tepals that surround the reproductive parts of the flower. The tepals are showy, mostly because of their size, but magnolia flowers are not particularly specialised to attract any one pollinator. While they may be visited by a number of different kinds of insects, pollination is mostly carried out by pollen-feeding beetles, which again is characteristic in primitive flowers. In bigleaf magnolia the huge flowers are composed of six broad tepals, the inner three purple-blotched at the base. The flowers are usually sparingly produced and often somewhat hidden in upper branches, but they make a spectacular display, contrasted against the expanded leaves.

Bigleaf magnolia leaves overwinter as miniature, unexpanded versions of themselves, tucked into finger-sized buds. A pair of bud scales – an inner and an outer – surround each bud. These are, technically speaking, stipules. In *Magnolia*, there is an enclosing pair of stipules on every emerging leaf. When they fall away, they leave a typical circular scar around the branch.

The expanded leaves – perhaps the bigleaf magnolia's most distinctive feature – are rippled and matte green, and sometimes up to a metre long on especially vigorous shoots. They are generally broadest above the middle, and more or less paddle-shaped. The leaves of all magnolias are spirally arranged on the stems and, in bigleaf magnolia, are more or less clustered at the tips of branches, radiating like enormous parasols. Although this arrangement looks perfectly appropriate on a gigantic tree, it can create a particularly unwieldy, even hilarious-looking effect on a young, single-stemmed tree. Both the new stems and the leaf undersides are coated in a white powdery wax, and because of this white bloom, a tree in full leaf viewed from below can look spectacular against a blue sky. It is often remarked that when they fall to the ground in the autumn the leaves don't require raking, as they are so large that they are more easily gathered up by hand. Regardless of the playful hyperbole, there is a coarse majesty to bigleaf magnolia that only strengthens as the tree grows.

To physically support such a large leaf and to efficiently supply moisture to all of its living cells is no small task for the bigleaf magnolia. The architecture of the veins must therefore be both strong and intricate, exploiting the whole interior of the blade. Magnolia leaves of all kinds have considerable lignin in their veins to accomplish this. Lignin is the compound that makes wood tough and resistant. Spanning the space between the veins of the leaf are green tissues primarily composed of cellulose, the material that makes a celery stalk stiff. Note, however, that compared with a woody twig, celery is both easily chewed and digested. Leave a magnolia leaf on the ground over the winter, and the vein architecture will be slowly exposed as the green cellulosic tissues are gradually eaten away by unseen microorganisms, while the lignin-rich scaffold of veins persists. In less than a year, a magnolia leaf can be transformed from a stiff green blade to a delicate filigree skeleton, much adored and collected by children and those who are craft-inspired.

GIANT SEAGRAPE

Coccoloba gigantifolia

Of the world's 60,000 or so known dicotyledonous tree species, the giant seagrape of the Brazilian Amazon has the largest leaves. From short, stout leaf stems come broad, egg-shaped blades that are up to an impressive 2.5 metres long and nearly 1.5 metres wide. Deep green above and paler beneath, these are somewhat leathery in texture, with wavy margins, and short hairs along the veins above and more generally across the back of the leaf. A small understorey tree, its flowers are inconspicuous but are followed by grape-like fruits, which, in some other species of seagrape (there are around 150), can be eaten. The name *Coccoloba* is derived from the Greek *kokkolobis* – a kind of grape, translated literally as 'berry pod'. The vernacular name 'seagrape', used for all *Coccoloba* species, relates to the coastal habitats of most member of the genus. Seagrapes are not to be confused with sea grapes, species of green algae – seaweeds – belonging to the genus *Caulerpa*, which are sometimes used in salads in east Asia and Oceania.

Coccolobas are known for their outsized leaves, but they also display a leaf feature that identifies them as members of the buckwheat family, Polygonaceae. Surrounding the leaf base is a sheath known as an ochrea (sometimes ocrea), which helps protect the leaves as they develop. This is formed by the fusion of a pair (or more) of stipules that subtend the leaf. The word ochrea comes from Latin and roughly means 'greave'. Greaves are, in history, pieces of substantial, all-round leg armour worn by warriors going into battle. Ochreas serve a similar function of protecting the leaf, though they are rather more papery, or leaf-like, in texture. Poor protection from flailing swords, but otherwise successful in the buckwheat family.

With a near-global distribution and comprising around 1,200 species in nearly 50 genera, the buckwheats are well-known for their medicinal qualities, and several seagrapes are extensively used in traditional folk medicine. Those living in temperate climes are perhaps most familiar with the buckwheat family member dock leaves (*Rumex* species), whose leaves are renowned for their use in treating stings from the European stinging nettle (*Urtica dioica*) and for treating skin problems more generally. As well as buckwheat itself (*Fagopyrum esculentum*), the family also includes rhubarb (*Rheum rhabarbarum* and *R. rhaponticum*), which, though they are not trees, have impressive leaf stems that are perfection in a crumble.

Among the seagrapes are several other large-leaved trees, though in those, oversized leaves tend to be more associated with vigorous, juvenile growth. Oversized leaves in juvenility or in response to pruning or other damage is a not uncommon phenomenon across the plant kingdom, with Indian bean tree (*Catalpa bignonioides*, see page 277) and foxglove tree (*Paulownia tomentosa*) among the most extreme woody examples that occur in the temperate world.

Giant seagrape, though, like all seagrapes, hails from the wet neotropics (American tropics), where large leaves are common among all types of plant. In the Amazon Basin, where moisture is plentiful, leaves can keep themselves cool via evapotranspiration, and can thus afford to be larger.

While the size of a leaf for the most part determines its photosynthetic potential, the availability of moisture and nutrients influences to what extent a big leaf can develop. But exposure to sunshine also has an influence on the biological success of a particular leaf size. As with teak, another large-leaved tropical, this is because a large leaf surface area exposed to sunlight will heat up, and without some way to moderate the heating, the temperature may continue to rise beyond what is optimal for photosynthesis or, indeed, the health of the leaf tissues. Large leaves can develop deep lobing or holes (like the Swiss cheese plant, *Monstera deliciosa*) to help with radiating heat away, but another alternative is heavy shade, and this is how the giant seagrape survives in its rainforest home.

Of course, having larger leaves mean that you need fewer of them, and specimens of giant seagrape seldom have more than a handful. A trade-off is made by the tree, it being cheaper to invest its energy in leaf size rather than in producing more wood, though the costs of making large leaves is in itself by no means insignificant.

Perhaps surprisingly given its unprecedently large leaves, the giant seagrape is only a recent discovery and was only formally published as a species in 2019. It was first encountered along the Canumã River in the Brazilian Amazon by botanists in 1982. Other observations were subsequently made toward the end of that decade, but because the first observed specimens were in fruit but without flowers, it was not possible to determine whether the specimens represented a new or an existing species. It was thus required to sow seeds and grow the plants until they produced flowers and fruits – the necessary material by which to determine the species.

With gigantic leaves, preparing herbarium vouchers is no simple task. For the giant seagrape, instead of using conventional drying ovens, which are built to dry more 'usual'-sized specimens, 3-metre-long presses were specially constructed and the leaves dried using an air conditioner. They were then mounted and put on display at the National Institute of Amazonian Research for the public to marvel at.

New discoveries in the Amazon are not uncommon. A two-year survey over 2014 and 2015 identified more nearly 400 previously undocumented species, with over half of them being plants. Rainforests are centres of biodiversity and those in the tropics are home to around half of the world's plants and animals. Around 16,000 of the world's 60,000 tree species are found in the Amazon, with discoveries still to be made and species to describe.

Depressingly though, it has become a race to describe them before they go extinct. An astonishing one-sixth of the Amazon's land area has been converted from rainforest in the last 50 years. Trees are being lost as a result of relentless logging and increased incidence of fire, and vast swathes of the Amazon now receive far less rain than in the past, owing to a rapidly changing climate and to the effects of deforestation itself. It is estimated that a 20–25 per cent loss of trees is the tipping point that would start to change the Amazon from its present character of closed-canopy rainforest to open savannah. Unsurprisingly, the small populations of giant seagrape were considered threatened with extinction as soon as they were described. The species might be lucky to become more than a museum exhibit.

SACRED FIG

Ficus religiosa

Capable of developing a trunk of house-size dimensions, sacred fig is most definitely a tree, though it often begins life as an epiphyte, growing in the crown of another tree, before sending roots down to the ground. These roots penetrate the host tree's stem and grow down through the trunk, eventually splitting it apart and establishing itself as a tree in its own right. Though the sacred fig is sometimes classified as a strangler fig, technically it is not. Strangler figs produce roots that smother and squeeze the host tree from the outside; although it makes little difference what we call it, as the host is sacrificed either way.

As well as trees and stranglers, *Ficus*, the fig genus, also includes a wide variety of climbers, shrubs and creepers. There are species that grow without soil on the surface of rocks (lithophytes) and even aquatic plants that grow along fast-flowing watercourses (rheophytes).

The sacred fig is native to large parts of the Indian subcontinent and South-East Asia. In South Asia it is mentioned in several ancient religious texts and is considered the holiest of trees. Capable of living for well over 1,000 years, sacred figs are often associated with shrines, and they retain great significance for Buddhists, Hindus and Jains. It was beneath a sacred fig in Bodh Gaya (in present day Bihar state), northeast India, that Siddhartha Gautama, the Buddha, is said to have attained enlightenment. While a temple marks the spot, the original tree is no longer there, though the offspring of another sacred fig is. The current tree at Bodh Gaya was grown from one in Anuradhapura in Sri Lanka, which itself was rooted from a branch of the tree the Buddha is recorded as having meditated beneath. The Anuradhapura tree, dating from 288 BCE, is reputed to be the oldest planted tree in the world, and this, as well as the tree in Bodh Gaya and other ancient specimens, is a prominent site of pilgrimage for Buddhists.

Sacred figs that can be traced back to the original tree in Bodh Gaya are known as bodhi trees. *Ficus religiosa* trees in commerce also often carry that name, but religious authorities condemn the use of the name bodhi for unauthenticated specimens. There is no shortage of alternatives, however, as the species has more than 150 common names in over 35 languages. Along with its spiritual significance, local names often relate to the tree's extensive use in traditional medicine, as all parts of the plant have long been used to treat a range of ailments, including respiratory, digestive and sexual disorders.

Largely thanks to its venerable status, sacred fig has been introduced to other regions that enjoy warm climates, such as other parts of Asia, Africa and the Americas. The species is widely grown and shared via cuttings and seeds, but is now considered invasive in parts of the United States and the Pacific region. Like all figs, it is reliant on a specific pollinator-wasp to reproduce in the wild and, like the plant, the sacred fig wasp (*Blastophaga quadraticeps*) has also found its way to new places, facilitating the tree's reproduction in new environs.

A remarkable tree, certainly, and we've not yet even mentioned the leaves. Frequently depicted in artwork, films and even on clothing, the leaves are readily identified by their heart-shaped blades. These are held on slender, flattened petioles – though by far their most distinguishing character is their impressively long tails, which dangle at the tip of the blade, making up around half of its length.

There are several botanical terms that describe the variation displayed by leaf tips. Those that are blunt are labelled 'obtuse', while leaf tips that are pointed are termed 'acute'. Longer tips warrant the term 'acuminate', from the Latin *acumen*, which means 'sharp'. Still longer points are 'attenuate' (i.e. narrowed to a point), and long, tail-like tips are described as 'caudate'. Caudate should not be confused with 'cordate', which translates as 'heart-shaped' and is used to describe a leaf base with rounded lobes on either side of the petiole. Sacred fig leaves are then, in fact, both cordate and caudate. Tail-like leaf tips are generally referred to as 'drip-tips' and few trees have drip-tips as striking as those of the sacred fig.

What drip-tips actually do is simple enough to understand: they accelerate the removal of water from the leaf surface. But why do that? There are several potential ecological advantages in having drip-tips, and plant scientists have long pondered the possibilities. There seems to be no one simple answer, but there are plenty of theories. A popular one is that rapid water removal limits colonisation of the leaf surface by organisms such as algae and lichens whose presence would reduce the interception of light. When relying on sunlight to make your food, you don't want someone drawing the curtains. Disease-causing (pathogenic) fungi and bacteria are also more likely to gain a foothold the longer a film of water persists on the leaf surface. Another theory goes that a coating of water on a leaf could limit transpiration by obstructing the stomata and thus reduce the plant's ability to take up nutrients from the soil, though this one hardly seems likely for the sacred fig, as its stomata are only located on the drier undersides of the leaves. More plausible, perhaps, is that the weight of excess water may require investment in additional structural support (i.e. in stronger leaves and branches). There is another theory, which is not to do with the leaf's ability to shed water quickly after rainfall, but more about its role while it is still raining. It has been suggested that, as the water droplets falling from leaves with long drip-tips are smaller than droplets from those with short ones, this might alleviate the threat of splash-induced soil erosion at the base of the tree. Though trees with long drip-tips are common in areas where soils are prone to erosion, results of testing this particular hypothesis have to date proved inconclusive.

Plants with drip-tips are particularly prevalent in the wetter regions of the tropics. That association has led to drip-tips being regarded as an indicator of historical rainforest conditions in palaeoecological reconstructions of past climates. An interesting observation is that, in a rainforest setting, trees with drip-tips are generally smaller than those without them. In some species, at least, the length of the drip-tip decreases with age, as the tree increases in size. The explanation is that leaves exposed to more sunlight and wind dry quicker, and hence have no need of long drip-tips.

And though long drip-tipped species are predominantly tropical, temperate species do have leaves with drip-tips, probably for some of the same reasons. Linden, or lime trees (*Tilia*), as well as species of birch (*Betula*) and hornbeam (*Carpinus*) are a few common examples. They are just neither as long, nor as impressive. But then, without the heat and humidity of the tropical forest, the incidence of foliar pathogens and epiphytes is not as great, so the need to dry the leaves in a hurry is also not as critical.

BRAZILIAN FERN TREE

Schizolobium parahyba

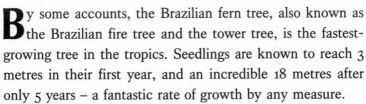

By some accounts, the Brazilian fern tree, also known as the Brazilian fire tree and the tower tree, is the fastest-growing tree in the tropics. Seedlings are known to reach 3 metres in their first year, and an incredible 18 metres after only 5 years – a fantastic rate of growth by any measure.

The Brazilian fern tree is native to open-forested situations from southern Mexico to as far south as southern Brazil. The Paraíba do Norte (Parahyba) River, for which this tree is named, is located in north-eastern Brazil. In the wild, trees are straight-trunked and often have magnificent flange-like buttressed bases, especially in shallow soils. The species tends to inhabit areas with well-defined wet and dry seasons, but its rapid growth and tolerance of low-fertility soils make it ideal for erosion control and restoring tropical woodlands, so it is widely planted. And because the shade it produces is light and even, trees are sometimes interspersed with coffee plants on plantations.

As impressive as these trees are, rapid growth in most trees is linked with a shortened lifespan and Brazilian fern trees in the wild seldom live longer than 40 years. Live fast and die young, as they say. The timber, which is soft and lightweight, was traditionally used for dugout canoes, but because of its poor durability, it is nowadays seldom used for anything other than packing crates, particleboard, or pulp for paper. Trees are celebrated nevertheless, but not just for their towering growth and productivity. The crown of a mature *Schizolobium* can appear as if completely engulfed in fiery yellow flowers when in full bloom, hence its being known as Brazilian fire tree. The tree has also been compared with jacaranda (*Jacaranda mimosifolia*), which is renowned for its floral extravagance. In parts of Australia, for example, *Schizolobium* is known as yellow jacaranda. Not only are the flowers spectacular, but the nectar reportedly produces a clear, deliciously fragrant honey.

Brazilian fern tree is a member of Fabaceae – the pea family – which is a huge assemblage of plants. It is the third largest family of land plants, with some 19,000 species, distributed across all the habitable continents. Like in most other peas, the leaves of the Brazilian fern tree are formed of multiple leaflets and are thus considered compound leaves. In pinnate- or feather-compound leaves, individual leaflets are arranged along a central axis, like the barbs in a feather or the leafy parts of a fern frond. The leaves of *Schizolobium* are twice-pinnate, which means that the leaflets are borne on the secondary, not the primary, divisions of the leaf. In this species, these divisions are perpendicular to the central leaf axis. Pinnate, twice-pinnate and even thrice-pinnate leaves are all relatively common in the pea family. So, why are pinnately compound leaves so frequently encountered in the family, and especially in hot and sunny parts of the world? The simple answer is that compound leaves have the capacity to keep themselves cool. This works because very small, separate leaflets that are collected together can represent a large surface area, without accumulating the amount of heat that would be absorbed by a contiguous leaf surface of the same photosynthetic area. Pinnately compound peas also have another trick up their foliar sleeves, which is that the leaflets are conduplicate. In other words, each leaflet has the ability to fold upwards, which means that in times of extreme heat or drought, the leaf surface exposed to the sun can be reduced to a minimum.

Rapidly growing, immature Brazilian fern trees with their slender, solitary, unbranched trunks can have leaves that are truly immense, each with thousands of individual leaflets. Radiating stiffly around the stems, the leaves look – especially when viewed from below and at a distance – remarkably like those of a palm tree or tree fern. As with nearly all trees, traditional cultures have found uses for the leaves of the Brazilian fern tree. Not unexpectedly for a tree with such plentiful leaves, it has been used as domestic animal forage, and the leaves have also been employed in traditional medicine. An example of this is teas made from *Schizolobium* leaves, which are believed to be effective in the treatment of colds and to remedy coughs. While the efficacy of tea made from fern-tree leaf is unsubstantiated by Western medicinal standards, the use of the leaves to make potent anti-venoms effective against at least two dangerously poisonous Brazilian pit-vipers has been well established.

As many people know, the pea family is characterised in part by a fruit known as a legume. The legume is one of the most recognisable of all botanical fruits, and is most often an elongated, cylindrical or flattened green pod with a single row of flattened seeds inside. Snap beans and peas-in-the-pod are familiar fruits (though they are generally known as vegetables), but not all legumes conform to this classic shape; nor are they all edible. The flattened, woody, coaster-sized fruit of the Brazilian fern tree would to most people be unrecognisable as a legume. It has an attractive teardrop shape and contains but a single, large seed. Like a typical ripe legume, it splits open along sutures on both sides to free the seed within. The genus name – from the Greek *schizo*, to divide, and *lobion*, a pod – is from the fact that the fruit splits into two identical halves when mature. As in most tropical forest trees, a large, energy-rich seed is necessary to help seedlings establish quickly and to push emerging stems upward through thick debris on the forest floor. While still in the tree, however, the fruits of the Brazilian fern tree attract birds, including the scarlet macaw (*Ara macao*), whose formidable beak makes short work of prising the immature legumes open to reach the nutritious seed locked inside. In the absence of seed-eating birds, the mature legume eventually breaks free of its attachment and falls, spinning eccentrically (imagine the trajectory of a table tennis paddle from the top of a tall building), before eventually landing on the ground. Ideally the seed is deposited well away from the shade of the parent tree, and in this, with such a wobbly flight path, the tree's great height and the possibility of a strong wind are advantageous.

TASMANIAN TREE FERN

Dicksonia antarctica

Ferns are normally associated with cool woodland walks. A ferny stem suggests a fine filigree of delicate foliage, while a ferny bower calls to mind a lush, knee-high massing of ferns in the dappled light of elegant, spreading trees. People, at least those in the Northern Hemisphere, seldom think of a fern as a tree; but imagine a different sort of ferny forest walk – admittedly, a warmer, drippier one – with ferns that *are* the forest.

This is the world of the Tasmanian tree fern, a native of Australia's humid south-eastern coast, from south-eastern Queensland to the island of Tasmania. This provenance is what gives the species its name, *antarctica*, which means 'southern', as well as its common name. The impressively dense canopy of overlapping, radiating fronds is supported on thick, fibrous stalks that are themselves home to hundreds or perhaps even thousands of other organisms – animals and epiphytes from the small to the minuscule and microscopic eke out an existence between the folds and fibres of the tree fern's sponge-like trunk. Among the more visible residents are tiny orchids, ferns and mosses. Even the root mat below the trunk is home to animals. For example, the endangered Narracan burrowing crayfish (*Engaeus phyllocercus*), an inch-long red or purple crustacean, spends most of its life underground beneath *Dicksonia antarctica* and other tree ferns in wet gullies in Victoria.

If a forest of Tasmanian tree ferns brings to mind a prehistoric scene, the image is probably a mostly accurate one. First appearing in the fossil record at about 187 million years ago, tree ferns have been around for nearly twice as long as the flowering plants. Dinosaurs would have been regular companions (if not diners). Tasmanian tree fern is not the most impressive of the tree ferns – the 20-metre-tall Norfolk Island tree fern, the largest fern in the world, has fronds that are bigger. But Tasmanian tree fern can grow to 15 metres tall and produce a crown that extends to nearly 6 metres in diameter, which is still pretty remarkable and speaks to the success of these ancient plants. Still, ferns are considered primitive or, at least, less broadly successful than the seed plants, and this is exhibited in a number of ways. As large as tree ferns can be, like all ferns they lack the internal mechanics to produce stems that could support a truly tree-sized canopy of branches, as the flowering plants and conifers do with wood. And because ferns reproduce from spores, rather than seeds, they are limited in the variety of environments that they can exploit. Spores are not particularly long-lived, nor capable of germinating without an abundance of water, which is why ferns are more common in wet places and nearly absent from drier ones. Given plentiful moisture, however, ferns have got shade worked out.

As with all ferns, the leaves of the Tasmanian tree fern are known as fronds. They are as spectacular in their unfurling as they are efficient in their photosynthetic coverage. From each spirally arranged, ascending and arching stipe (leaf stem), a frond radiates perfectly outward from the crown, the tight rows of primary segmentations, called pinnae (from the Latin *penni*, for feather), drooping slightly to the sides. Each primary division of a fern frond is known by the singular word pinna. Many ferns bear pinnae in just this way, with two simple rows, one on either side of an unbranched axis. The indoor Boston fern (*Nephrolepis exaltata* 'Bostoniensis'), and polypodies (*Polypodium* species), a familiar constituent of forests across the Northern Hemisphere, both produce fronds that look like this. In *Dicksonia*, each pinna is divided a second time, with a set of leafy pinnules borne down either side of the pinna's stalk. The margins of each of these pinnules is deeply lobed, such that the pinnae appear to mirror the whole frond in miniature. In some ferns, these ultimate segments may be divided again, with their own tinier stalks – thus, into pinnulules (yes, that's what they're called) – and even, incredibly, to smaller, fourth-order divisions. At each order of division, the space between the segments becomes smaller, such that the photosynthetic surface is increasingly optimised. A fern frond is also seen as a model of self-similarity, where a similar pattern is exhibited at increasingly smaller scales. In mathematics, these patterns are known as fractals, and the unfolding symmetry of the fern's crozier (its fiddlehead) is frequently used to represent them.

Tasmanian tree fern, like other tree ferns, grows from a tough stem known as a rhizome. The rhizome is a common feature of all kinds of ferns, but in non-arborescent ferns it is typically an underground structure that seldom elongates much at all. Nearly all familiar temperate woodland ferns follow this pattern, although in a few, like bracken (*Pteridium aquilinum*) and the polypody, the rhizome is a creeping structure that roots as it goes – underground for bracken and crawling along the surface for the polypody. Around any fern rhizome are borne the fronds, their undersides frequently spotted with spore cases in regular patterns. On the Tasmanian tree fern there is a single, hemp-seed-shaped spore case at the edge of each lobe on the pinnule. Although a spore case is about 1 millimetre in diameter, each one contains between 600 and 800 spores, and a mature Tasmanian tree fern is capable of producing some tens of millions of spores each year.

The stipe of a fern frond, as anyone who has handled one knows, is usually fibrous and very tough, particularly toward its base, and the stipes are often accompanied by shaggy, fibrous hairs. Fern fronds are spirally arranged and often packed tightly together. In a tree fern, the stipe bases are accompanied by a dense layer of aerial roots and long hairs, and all persist after the fronds have deteriorated. This results in a thick ruff that protects the rhizome inside. The roots also allow the tree fern to re-establish if the trunk falls over and becomes uprooted, or even in the unlikely event that the crown becomes severed from its trunk. In *D. antarctica*, the stipe bases almost disappear into the mass of soft brown hairs and aerial roots, which is the derivation of the common name in Australia – soft tree fern. Although the species is more prevalent on the continent, the evocative 'Tasmanian tree fern' is the more common moniker outside of Australia.

DAWN REDWOOD

Metasequoia glyptostroboides

M ost, but not all, conifers are evergreen. And among those that are not are some of the most eye-catching trees in the temperate world. Deciduous species are found in only two conifer families. The pine family, Pinaceae, has the larches (*Larix* species). They are known for their timber, but also their stunning yellow autumn colour, which is bettered perhaps only by a close relative, the golden larch (*Pseudolarix amabilis*). Golden larch, as the name suggests, turns stunning shades of gold before dropping its leaves for the winter.

The remainder of the deciduous conifers belong in the cypress family, Cupressaceae, but the three species – each in its own genus – stand apart foliage-wise, compared with the familiar evergreen cypresses used for hedging. Each has fine, needle-shaped leaves borne on deciduous branchlets. Those of the bald cypresses of the United States and Mexico, varieties of *Taxodium distichum*, and of the Chinese swamp cypress (*Glyptostrobus pensilis*), hold their branchlets alternately along the stem. The branchlets of dawn redwood, in contrast, are oppositely arranged. Like the larches, these species also have exceptional autumn leaf colour, adopting orange and bronze hues before dropping.

So, why are some trees deciduous and others evergreen? Unsurprisingly, it has to do with how species have adapted to succeed in their natural environments. Where conditions are favourable for growth all year round, such as in the wet tropics, plants will mostly be evergreen. Here, there is little cause for leaves to be shed en masse, as they can function throughout the year. Under such conditions, evergreen trees often produce robust leaves that persist for several years. In seasonal climates where there is a dry or frigid period, on the other hand, it is often biologically advantageous to produce thin leaves that can be quickly discarded. But as might be expected, life strategies often differ profoundly among species. Some temperate-climate understorey species opt for evergreen leaves so that they can benefit from the increased light in spring and autumn when there are fewer leaves on the trees above, but these leaves have to be especially tough and frost-resistant. While most temperate broad-leaved evergreen plants are able to photosynthesise in low light levels, deciduous trees operating in higher-light environments are not.

In the case of the dawn redwood, mummified *Metasequoia* leaves found in the leaf litter layer of fossil forests on Axel Heiberg Island, in Arctic Canada, illustrate that species in the genus once grew further north than any tree does today. At least three species of *Metasequoia* are known to have existed in the past, and it is possible that more than one grew on Axel Heiberg Island alongside species of *Glyptostrobus*, larch, hickory (*Carya*), katsura and birch. A curious mix of animals occurred here too, including crocodilians, turtles and an extinct, huge rhinoceros-like herbivore, *Megacerops*. This eclectic assemblage points to a time when there was a warm temperate climate near the North Pole, and while in the summer the high light levels would have been optimal for tree growth, the dark winters would not have been. Thus, a winter deciduous habit would have been advantageous, and one which the genus, now down to a single representative, has since retained.

The discovery of the dawn redwood as a living plant was one of the greatest botanical events of the twentieth century. In 1941 a Japanese paleobotanist, Shigeru Miki (1901–1974), found fossils of a previously unknown redwood-like conifer, which he named *Metasequoia*. Miki apparently found the fossils in rocks where he had first seen impressions of material belonging to the coast redwood genus, *Sequoia*, hence the name *Metasequoia*: from the Greek *meta* = after or beyond + *Sequoia*. These fossils were from the Mesozoic, and more than 150 million years old, while this 'new' genus was thought to have gone extinct more than 1.5 million years ago.

In 1943 or 1944, a Chinese researcher, Chan Wang (1911–2000), who was travelling across central China, learned of a strange tree located in the small village of Moudao, Hubei, and made a detour to collect material from it. Without proper study of it, the material was deposited in a herbarium and determined as belonging to the Chinese swamp cypress (*Glyptostrobus pensilis*).

Three years later, further samples were sent to the distinguished Chinese botanist Professor Wan Chun Cheng, who discussed them with his colleague, Professor Hu Hsien Hsu (1994–1968), who was renowned for his knowledge of Chinese flora. Hu Hsien Hsu was familiar with the paleobotanical work of Shigeru Miki and recognised that the samples belonged to Miki's *Metasequoia* genus; in 1948, together with Wan Chun Cheng, he named the specimens as the new species *Metasequoia glyptostroboides*, acknowledging the species' resemblance to the Chinese swamp cypress (*glyptostroboides* = '*glyptostrobus*-like'). It was dubbed a 'living fossil' by media reports of the day and given the name 'dawn redwood' by the *San Francisco Chronicle* reporter who went to China to report on its discovery.

At the time of its discovery, the original, living dawn redwood specimen was surrounded by a shrine, and villagers referred to it as *shui-shan* or 'water fir', denoting its occurrence in damp habitats, much like its deciduous cupressaceous relatives. This specimen is now over 400 years old, and though the species doesn't quite reach the great heights of the Californian redwoods, it is assumed capable of growing to at least 50 metres tall. Introduced to the West in 1948, specimens in botanic gardens were quick off the mark, growing vigorously and becoming reproductive within a few short years. None of these first introductions, nor any of their offspring, have quite reached their assumed maximum height, but two originals (both at Longwood Gardens in Pennsylvania, US) are now over 40 metres tall. Dawn redwood has become a popular tree and is also common in urban areas, its delicate foliage and upright form well suited to restricted conditions, while it is evidently also pollution-tolerant.

The species is also a record holder; in Jiangsu Province, China, a staggering one million trees line 47 kilometres of main road through Pizhou County, the world's longest avenue. While its wild populations are restricted, and the species is listed as Endangered on the IUCN Red List, its popularity bodes well for a positive future.

GINKGO

Ginkgo biloba

For many, the image of a gingko leaf is more recognisable than the tree itself. Likenesses of their familiar fan shape are widely used in the interior design world, from wallpapers to fabrics, art prints to earrings, ornaments to tattoos. Noted for their unique shape, the leaves, along with the tree itself, are said to symbolise longevity, hope and peace.

The leaves of ginkgo are unique not only for their form, but also for their distinctive venation, with veins that radiate from the base, sometimes splitting, but never forming a network as occurs in most vascular plants. Hold a fresh leaf up to the light, and this character becomes immediately apparent.

Widely grown in the East, the name *Ginkgo* is thought to have come from the Japanese *gin kyo*, itself derived from the Chinese *yín xìng*, which translates as 'silver apricot', in reference to its globular fruit. An alternative common name, maidenhair tree, refers to the leaves, which resemble somewhat the leaflets of the European maidenhair fern (*Adiantum capillus-veneris*). The specific epithet *biloba* refers to the leaves often being more or less notched at the tip, and hence bi-lobed. This character is somewhat variable though, and some leaves are not at all lobed. From light green, these turn butter-yellow in autumn before swiftly falling, with individual trees often going from near-full crowns to leafless in the space of a few days, particularly following frost. Collections of fallen leaves often make eye-catching patterns on the ground beneath trees.

Though possessing broad leaves that are superficially like those of flowering plants, ginkgo is a gymnosperm, its reproductive structures bearing naked ovules.

The family, Ginkgoaceae – which consists of this species alone – sits closest to, though still some distance from, conifers, gnetophytes (primarily the joint-firs, *Ephedra*, and *Welwitschia*) and cycads on the evolutionary tree. Its fossils date from over 270 million years ago, when ginkgos occurred in North America, Europe, Australia and Asia. This was in a time when gymnosperms as a whole were far more diverse – flowering plants had not yet evolved. This group is now reduced to around 650 conifers, 350 cycads, 100 gnetophytes and a single *Gingko*; though the genus even in its heyday perhaps only comprised half a dozen species.

While the majority of gymnosperms bear cones, ginkgo does not, though its seeds are no less distinctive. Green in summer, they turn golden yellow when ripe, falling to the ground in autumn. The outer seed coating, the sarcotesta, begins to putrefy soon after making contact with the ground, producing an overwhelmingly strong, near retch-inducing odour. The smell, caused by butyric acid, increases when the fragile skins are bruised, so handling the seeds directly is best avoided, particularly as the stench can remain on the skin for hours regardless of washing. Handily, from a growing perspective, ginkgos are, however, usually dioecious, the male and female structures occurring on separate trees. Thus, preferred male clones can be identified and propagated, which is more or less standard procedure for ginkgos in the West. Only very rarely do male trees throw out a female branch – a handy adaptation to have in the race to survive, but potentially unlucky for the unsuspecting gardener. However, trees usually take between 20 and 30 years to mature, and seemingly take a lot longer before they might consider a sex change, which helps to minimise the chances of a particularly foul-smelling autumn. As to why ginkgo seeds smell as bad as they do, it is likely that some prehistoric animal was attracted by the stink. The seeds thus ingested would pass through the guts and germinate in a pile of suitable organic matter.

Roasted ginkgo seeds are prized in eastern Asia and are used there in traditional medicine to treat numerous ailments including respiratory, urinary and vaginal complaints. However, the seeds also contain chemicals similar to the compounds that cause allergic reactions to the varnish tree and its pistachio family relatives. Consumption causes problems usually only when consumed in excess, though responses vary from person to person. Vomiting or even loss of consciousness can occur in the hours after immoderate ingestion.

While in the East medicinal use of ginkgo revolves around its seeds (despite their evident toxicity), in the West an extract from the leaves is used as much, if not more widely, being promoted mainly as a memory improver. Supposed benefits come at least in part from flavonoids found within the leaf – multifunctional chemicals that influence flower colour and pathogen resistance, and that are themselves antioxidant compounds. The leaves are usually harvested when the flavonoid content is at its highest, just as they begin to turn from green to yellow in autumn, though leaves for another popular product, ginkgo tea, are harvested in spring.

Ginkgo leaf extract is mostly prescribed to elderly people as an aid to concentration and energy, as well as to treat depression and to boost learning capacity and even circulation. Health benefits surely come from the fact that terpenoids, another class of leaf chemicals, are vasodilators, medications that open (dilate) the blood vessels. Dilated blood vessels readily provide an increase of oxygen to the brain and other organs. Unlike over-consumption of the seeds, the extract has few recognised side effects. Ginkgo leaf extract is indeed one of the leading prescription medicines in parts of Europe and has also gained popularity in the United States. Despite this popularity though, its efficacy beyond increase in blood flow is difficult to prove, and its reputation among the scientific community is somewhat controversial.

Ginkgo trees themselves are as revered as the leaves are popular; the species has been cultivated in China, Korea and Japan for millennia. The species is often associated with Buddhist temples, where monstrous specimens of over 1,000 years old are known. Ginkgo has long been cultivated in the West too; it was introduced to the Netherlands in the early 1700s, from where it was spread across Europe and North America. The tree's tolerance of unforgiving urban environments has seen it become widely used as a street tree, and it is also impressively resistant to insects, fungal infection and even bomb blasts. Ginkgo specimens survived the Hiroshima atomic bomb dropped at the end of World War Two in 1945 and their seeds have been distributed around the world to grow ceremonial 'peace trees'.

Though now widely grown across temperate regions, ginkgo is exceedingly rare in the wild and until recently was even thought to be extinct. Assumed wild populations have however been identified in both eastern and south-western China, and it is possible that further natural stands may be found. Like all gymnosperms though, ginkgo is a survivor, its resilience a significant asset that has seen it endure more than most. And thanks to its popularity today, its future looks bright.

INTIMATE RELATIONSHIPS . . .

It is not the strongest of the species that survives,
nor the most intelligent that survives. It is the one that
is the most adaptable to change, that lives within the
means available and works cooperatively against
common threats.

CHARLES DARWIN

What often defines the best relationships in people is an under-standing of what's mutually valuable to the parties involved. This is not unlike the mutualism we observe in the plant world, though with plant–insect interactions there's no need for discussion; a few million years of evolution has typically honed these relationships to the point of exquisite efficiency. The plants grow, the insects set up shop in or on them and both prosper. The details, however, are what attract us to the associations, and often to the unexpected results of those finely tuned bonds. Figs, for instance, need wasps. (And where would we be without fig leaves? Naked and exposed.) With the leaves of embaúba, bullhorn acacia and Indian bean tree, ants are the primary tie-in, but they are definitely not the only animals involved in these fascinating ecologies. Trotroka and mopane do depend on their animal associates as much as the animals rely on the leaves of those species. Animals and leaves are bound to each other in an intricate dance, but is what we see the beginning, middle or final chapter in the relationship?

COMMON FIG

Ficus carica

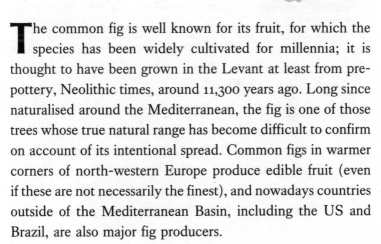

The common fig is well known for its fruit, for which the species has been widely cultivated for millennia; it is thought to have been grown in the Levant at least from pre-pottery, Neolithic times, around 11,300 years ago. Long since naturalised around the Mediterranean, the fig is one of those trees whose true natural range has become difficult to confirm on account of its intentional spread. Common figs in warmer corners of north-western Europe produce edible fruit (even if these are not necessarily the finest), and nowadays countries outside of the Mediterranean Basin, including the US and Brazil, are also major fig producers.

As well as its fruit, the leaves of the common fig have also long been recognised for their uses, including as a means of covering up. Adam and Eve are said to have 'sewed fig leaves together and made themselves loincloths' once they realised that they were naked (Genesis 3:7). During periods of excessive propriety, fig leaves have been used to preserve the modesty of nude figures in works of art. So shocked was Queen Victoria by the full-frontal nudity of the copy of Michelangelo's sculpture of David when she saw it at the Cast Courts of the Victoria and Albert Museum that Clemente Papi (1803–1875), who made the sculpture cast, was commissioned to make a cast of a fig leaf to cover the offending area. The cast, at half a metre high, would be hung from the sculpture, held on strategically placed hooks to conceal David's genitalia, to save the blushes of the queen and other visiting dignitaries.

The common fig is a member of the mulberry family, Moraceae, which contains approximately 1,180 species. Nearly three-quarters of them are figs. The figs are unified by their unique inflorescence, known as the syconium, which is a fleshy, hollow chamber that contains several minute flowers. Individual fig flowers are unisexual, and syconia can be strictly male or female, or hermaphrodite. Female flowers come in two forms: so-called gall flowers (which are short), and seed flowers (which are long). The gall flowers are parasitised by wasps, which lay their eggs in the ovaries, which then play host to the wasp larvae. In seed flowers, the wasp cannot reach the ovary or, so cannot disrupt normal seed production. In the common fig, inflorescences with male and gall flowers produce fruit that is dry and inedible; these are known as caprifigs – only those with seed flowers produce edible figs.

Though hugely significant in forest ecosystems and highly sought out by birds and primates, most figs are inedible to humans, the common fig being something of an exception in this respect. It is more so geographically, growing far away from the tropics where most other figs naturally occur. Several familiar figs are grown as houseplants, while climate change may soon see more species succeeding in hitherto cooler areas.

The common fig is a tree of modest height, but spreads vegetatively, via root suckers, and can form plants that spread far wider than they are tall. Its leaves are deciduous and usually three- or five-lobed, though can also be unlobed. Their lobing is in fact unusual, as most other figs are decidedly unlobed. However, variable lobing within a species, and even within individual specimens, is often observed in other members of the mulberry family, including the mulberries (of the genus *Morus*) themselves. Common fig leaves are thick and on the upper surface are rough like sandpaper, covered in short, stiff hairs. Several selections of the common fig have been made, usually for their fruiting qualities, but differences in leaf shape among them are also often easily observed.

Like all figs, common figs possess latex in all their parts, though particularly in the leaves; this is easily observed by cutting through the leaf stem, or by breaking a leaf off where it joins the branch. Latex occurs in over 20,000 plant species in more than 40 plant families and is the primary constituent of natural rubber (though the popular houseplant *Ficus elastica* is known as the rubber plant, the commercial source of natural rubber comes from *Hevea brasiliensis*, of the spurge family, Euphorbiaceae). Held under pressure in secretory cells known as laticifers, latex oozes from fresh wounds and on exposure to air becomes sticky and coagulates, not unlike animal blood. Though in figs and several other plants it appears white, latex can run clear or be yellow, orange or even red, as occurs in *Cannabis sativa*. It is also used in chewing gum from *Manilkara* species, while lacquer is also derived from latex (see varnish tree, page 179).

Latex is exuded as a result of injury and its production is associated with plant defence against herbivory, as latex is frequently toxic to would-be predators. In common fig, compounds that prevent protein digestion have been identified, as well as enzymes that actively degrade chitin, an essential component of insects' guts as well as of the cell walls of pathogenic fungi. The role of latex, in at least some plants, is also to help prevent further infection from wounds. *Hevea brasiliensis* does both, producing latex that coagulates to seal wounds but can also gum up the mouths of any potential insect predators. In figs, it is supposed that the primary role of latex is in fact to facilitate quick wound healing rather than to deter herbivory. Achieving both is an impressive feat!

For people, exposure to latex can result in skin irritation, though fig latex has been employed as medicine from at least the tenth century CE. Antioxidant, antifungal and antiviral properties are all present in common figs, with several compounds found in their greatest quantity in latex in the leaves. Unsurprisingly, common fig leaves are also used as animal fodder. Perhaps slightly more surprisingly, in Algeria extracts from common fig latex and artichoke flower (*Cynara scolymus*) are used in the production of artisanal cheese.

MOPANE

Colophospermum mopane

Mopane is a shrubby to medium-sized tree that occurs over a wide area of southern and central Africa, where it often forms pure stands. One of the most valuable trees in the region, it is of ecological, economic and social significance. *Colophospermum* is a member of the pea family, Fabaceae, and the sole member of its genus. It has highly distinctive, butterfly-shaped leaves that are also sometimes likened to a camel's footprint. Like virtually all members of the pea family, the leaves are compound, made up of multiple leaflets. In mopane there are just two leaflets, and the leaves are thus, botanically, bifoliolate. While not unique in the family – bifoliolate leaves occur in the fabaceous orchid trees (*Bauhinia* species) as well – this leaf morphology is rare. The two mopane leaflets join at their base, and are held on a slender petiole, where there is also a tiny point – the remnant of a third, terminal leaflet. The vernacular name and specific epithet,

259

mopane, comes from the Zimbabwean Shona word for butterfly.

Mopane trees are dry-deciduous, dropping their leaves for the dry winter season. With the returning rains in spring, the leaves emerge reddish before turning green. As is typical with peas, the leaflets fold up to limit water loss via evapotranspiration in response to heat and wind. It is a useful mechanism for these trees, but leaflet folding reduces what little shade the tree can offer for passing animals or people. More significant to animals is the protein content of the leaves, which is high, even in those fallen from the tree. Mopane leaves are in fact a seasonal staple food of the African elephant (*Loxodonta africana*), and perhaps the reason why some mopane stands never seem to get beyond being shrubby, despite their potential arboreal dimensions.

Trees that are predated upon by large mammals commonly possess spines or thorns as deterrents to wholesale defoliation. Mopane trees, in contrast, avoid having their photosynthetic potential completely decimated by elephants using chemistry. In response to foliar attack, the trees react by sending a rich cocktail of phenols and tannins from their roots into the twigs, seed pods and leaves, which swiftly renders them unpalatable. And while effective enough at an individual level, mopane doesn't stop at this, but continues releasing chemicals into the air. These aromatic compounds warn neighbouring mopane trees that a foliar attack could be imminent, and in response the receiving trees send tannins into their leaves. It is quite the neighbourly phenomenon, but it doesn't always work out for the mopane colony, as the effectiveness of the aromatic warnings depends on how strongly and in which direction the wind is blowing. This critical detail is one that elephants have apparently become wise to, and while mopane trees are communicating downwind, the elephants move steadily upwind, enjoying at least a few leaves before they become too unappetising.

People's relationship to mopane is perhaps more intricate still, and involves another of the tree's leaf predators, the resident mopane moth (*Gonimbrasia belina*). These inhabit mopane trees in their thousands. At the end of winter, the moths lay their eggs on the leaves, which in turn hatch into larvae known as mopane worms. And extraordinary they are. Cigar-sized and adapted to detoxifying the chemical brew that deters elephants and other mammalian browsers, these 'worms' are able to feed voraciously. And while capable of defoliating entire trees, mopane moths are active only over a period of around six weeks, and this allows the tree time to recover before the annual cycle begins once more.

Greyish, speckled, hairy and somewhat spiny, mopane worms tend to be targets not for birds, but for humans. The caterpillars are rich in protein, fats and vitamins, and an important food source across large parts of Africa. Harvested from the wild, mopane worms are of great economic significance, and what was once a matter for local economies has become an international trade. The expanding industry has come at an environmental cost, however, seriously diminishing populations and resulting in larger trees being felled in attempts to harvest the arboreal caterpillars. Schemes to ensure sustainable harvest will doubtless become increasingly important.

Traditionally, mopane worms are preserved by boiling and salting. They are then sun-dried, or smoked for extra flavour. At the industrial scale, they are brined and tinned, and are widely available in southern African supermarkets. They are

The Lives of Leaves

eaten dry as a snack, soaked in sauce or added to stews, fried with vegetables or even added to maize porridge. Fresh mopane worms are also eaten by grazing animals and may even be 'hunted' by ageing lions in search of a quick and easy meal.

Mopane worms aren't the only 'products' from mopane trees either. Cocoons spun by another caterpillar that also strongly favours mopane trees, the African wild silk moth (*Gonometa rufobrunnea*), are harvested for their silk. The more common source of wild silk in Africa is from the related but less selective kalahari wild silk moth (*Gonometa postica*). Mopane trees also play host to the mopane psyllid (*Retroacizzia mopani*), a sap-sucking insect that lives exclusively off mopane leaves and produces so-called 'mopane manna', a sweet, wax-like coating on the leaves that is harvested and eaten by both humans and other primates.

Mopane leaves, and other plant parts, are also used extensively in traditional medicine. In parts of Africa, fibres from chewed leaves are used to stop bleeding wounds, while a decoction from the leaves is used to treat headaches. The roots and bark of the tree are used to treat digestive ailments and bleeding gums in people and swollen limbs in cattle. Mopane seeds have a distinctive pine-like smell, which is provided by the compound alpha-pinene, present in numerous conifers (one of the common names is turpentine tree), while other essential oils are extracted from it for medicinal purposes, as well as for perfumery. The seeds are also known for their antibacterial qualities, but it is their odd surface sculpturing, reminiscent of human intestines, that gives the genus its name (*colophospermum* means 'colon-bearing seeds').

Another vernacular name for the species is 'ironwood', on

account of its dense, hard wood. Incredibly tough and termite-resistant, it is also attractive and widely used for house building, furniture, ornaments and musical instruments. Mopane bark is used to make twine, while its twigs are used for toothbrushes. Few trees are as useful to people and wildlife as mopane, nor as biochemically cunning. If only elephants could forget.

TROTROKA

Dichaetanthera cordifolia

The melastome family, Melastomataceae, comprises a large assemblage of herbs, shrubs, climbers and trees, with more than 200 genera and nearly 5,000 species. Pan-tropical in its distribution, it has a centre of diversity in the tropical regions of the Americas, where it is represented by around two-thirds of its species. It also occurs in Africa, Asia and Oceania, with several species utilised for timber, ornament, dye and, in some cases, food. *Melastoma*, after which the family is named, translates as 'black mouth' and refers to the staining that eating fruits of some melastome species can cause. The most familiar of the melastomes for gardeners in temperate regions is a summer bedding plant. Princess flower (*Tibouchina urvilleana*) is often treated like a standard fuchsia; that is, bedded out in the summer and overwintered in a warm greenhouse. It is a distinctive shrub with bold, velvety leaves and large, unforgettably rich-purple, flowers.

While in many cases in the plant kingdom the presence of flowers and fruit is required to determine to which family a plant belongs, melastomes have such distinct leaf characters that they can easily be identified by those features alone. The classic melastome leaf is borne in opposite pairs, in a decussate arrangement with each pair at right angles to the set above and below. Two to nine prominent, primary veins arise from the base on either side of the midrib, arching outwards and then gradually converging at the apex, with several smaller, parallel veins perpendicular to them. These secondary veins appear remarkably ladder-like, and are geometrically pleasing to the eye. Floral characters are slightly more variable, though most melastomes have deep-hued pink, purple, red or occasionally white flowers, with prominent stamens that are often tipped with very large anthers.

Given the floristic diversity on Madagascar, it is perhaps unsurprising that melastomes are so well represented there. The island is home to an impressive 12 genera and 321 species. Consistent with Madagascar's astounding rate of endemism, three of these genera and 317 species occur nowhere else. While endemism in plant species in Madagascar stands at around 80 per cent, within the Melastomataceae it is even higher, at an incredible 98 per cent.

The genus *Dichaetanthera*, while not wholly endemic to Madagascar, has its centre of diversity on the island, with 28 of its 35 species occurring there and nowhere else. Those not found on Madagascar are native to parts of Africa.

The most well-known *Dichaetanthera* species is *D. cordifolia*, known locally as trotroka, or alternatively tsingotrika. A diminutive tree, or sometimes only a shrub, it is recognised by its rounded to heart-shaped leaf base with five to seven characteristic veins arising from the base. The epithet *cordifolia* denotes the heart-shaped – cordate – leaf base, which is predominant especially on the leaves of vigorous stems. Like in all melastomes, the leaves are arranged oppositely along the stems, and the outermost primary veins run close to the leaf margins. The stems and leaf stems are covered in a golden pubescence and there are tiny scales on the lower leaf surfaces, similar to tufts of hairs. Trotroka occurs in central and eastern parts of Madagascar and sheds its leaves during the dry season to help prevent water loss. While deciduousness is rare in eastern Malagasy rainforests, it is the prevalent mechanism further west on the island, where the dry forests are without appreciable moisture from May until September. Pink and white flowers are produced in conical clusters at the tips of the branches soon after the leaves have expanded near at beginning of the rainy season.

Like all melastomes, trotroka is typically attractive in leaf and flower, though the species is certainly most notable for its relationship with a remarkable insect, the giraffe weevil (*Trachelophorus giraffa*), which, like its host, is a Madagascan endemic. A sexually dimorphic species, its vernacular name, as well as its specific epithet, *giraffa*, refers to the unusually long neck of the male. This is around twice the length of its body and two to three times the length of the neck of the female. This adaptation is thought to be useful in nest-building, but is also used for fighting, as rival males compete for the attention of females.

Not only does the weevil feed on the leaves of trotroka, but females also lay their eggs on it in a particularly intricate process. The female first clips veins in the leaf, making small creases in it. After mating, she begins to fold and roll the leaf, which is several times her size, using her legs, and finishes by curling up the end. Here, within the curl, she has laid a single egg. With egg enclosed, the female cuts the leaf from the tree, where it falls to the forest floor. After hatching, the larva eats the leaf that surrounded it throughout its development, before emerging as an adult weevil.

A second species, *Dichaetanthera arborea*, is also utilised by the giraffe weevil, but no other plants are known to support its reproduction. These two species are the only plants where conditions are right for the weevil to make her nest. They are also in a minority of plants on Madagascar not currently considered to be threatened with extinction. Given the complete reliance of the giraffe weevil on its melastome hosts, were the species to be lost, you could count on the weevil swiftly following.

EMBAÚBA

Cecropia pachystachya

Biodiversity can challenge a plant. All that competition for water, light and space, and the fending off of diseases and pests, can be pretty rough going. Like tropical forests everywhere, those of central and eastern South America, where embaúba is native, are among the most varied and biologically rich of terrestrial environments anywhere. But in these biodiverse settings the pressures against survival are monumental. There's always something trying to have you for lunch.

Cecropia are tropical trees in the nettle family, Urticaceae, native to tropical South and Central America and the Caribbean. There are some 60 species in the genus, all instantly recognisable. Their stems are strongly upright and mostly unbranched, except for a few, candelabra-like branches toward the top of the tree. They produce huge leaves, circular in outline, that are divided into up to twenty broad, palmate lobes that are rounded at the lobe tips. The petiole attaches close to the centre of the leaf – a peltate leaf attachment. Although the leaves are arranged oppositely along the stems, they radiate evenly and umbrella-like around the stem tips.

Embaúba, the Brazilian name for these trees, is somewhat typical of this pattern. It is a tree that grows to 25 metres tall in moist forests that span northern Argentina, Paraguay and southern Brazil. Young seedlings have leaves with a few broad lobes and comparatively shallow sinuses (the gaps between the lobes). At this age, they look a little like those of the common Japanese aralia (*Fatsia japonica*) but older trees gradually develop larger leaves, up to 60 centimetres across. Mature leaves have more numerous lobes and deeper sinuses, as well as significantly longer petioles. The leaves are glossy green above, but the petioles and leaf undersides are covered with a vestiture of creamy-white hairs. At the base of the petiole is a pair of specialised persistent stipules known as trichiliae. In most plants that bear them, stipules are leafy, green, usually paired appendages that fall away as the leaves expand. In embaúba, the triangular trichiliae are covered in a suede-like pelt of short, brownish hairs and lie flat against the petiole base. Among the hairs are tiny, whitish structures, modified hairs known as Müllerian bodies. While barely noticeable, these club-shaped hairs are common to nearly all cecropias, and figure prominently in the success of these trees.

Cecropia are dioecious – that is, there are separate male and female trees – and primarily wind-pollinated. Female trees produce sweet-fleshed fruits, readily taken by a wide range of birds and mammals, including sloths and bats; animals are the primary dispersers of the seeds. Embaúba is a pioneer species, adapted to growing in disturbed, open sites. Fast growing, the tree produces a relatively narrow crown that doesn't cast much shade, at least initially, allowing other plants to establish and grow around it. Embaúba can be relatively short-lived if overtaken by surrounding plants, as it is a shade-intolerant species. If allowed to develop to its full potential, however, it can become a valuable timber tree, yielding large volumes of lightweight, easily worked wood. In many plants a pioneering ecology, together with copiously produced, animal-dispersed seeds, often indicates a potential to become invasive. While not as damaging and capacious as a few other *Cecropia* species (*C. peltata* in particular), embaúba is now increasingly recognised as an invasive weed on a number of tropical islands, including Hawaii, Singapore and Java.

The leaves of embaúba are much used in traditional medicine. A tea made from the leaves is considered effective for upper respiratory problems and to help soothe sores in the mouth. The tea is also reputed to lower blood sugar; hence, it is a common folk remedy for diabetes. Whole leaves, which are used as wrappings for bruises and more serious wounds, are said to have pain-relieving, antiseptic and anti-inflammatory effects, as well. Trees produce a sticky, corrosive mucilage that is a topical treatment for warts and calluses, and is also harvested locally to make glue. The mucilage is produced primarily in the branch tips and is somewhat effective in protecting the buds from herbivory (sloths, primarily). Cures and treatments using different parts of the tree are numerous, but Western medicine has yet to corroborate their efficacy.

While the arborescent habit and leaf shape of embaúba are distinctive, these features are not particularly emblematic of Urticaceae. The nettle family is better known for stinging hairs, as in the common stinging nettle (*Urtica dioica*; and see giant stinging tree, page 173). Cecropias have no such hairs with which to protect themselves, but there is something else that does. Embaúba, like nearly all cecropias, is myrmecophilous: it is an ant-plant. Stinging ants in the genus *Azteca* associate with cecropias, providing protection from foliage-feeding insects, and even clip the wandering stems of climbers that might happen to be lying across a leaf. The ants vigorously defend the plants from all comers. Myrmecophily means 'ant-loving', but you could say the feeling is mutual. But why?

Cecropias and ants have co-evolved to benefit each other. First, the Müllerian bodies produced on the trichiliae provide the ants with a ready source of protein, fat and sugar. These food rewards are continuously produced as long as the trichiliae remain attached, but only when *Azteca* ants are present. Small, light-coloured spots on the stems near the trichiliae indicate points known as prostomata where the stem wall is weak. Here, the ants make a hole so that they can break into the hollow internal cavity to establish colonies. Were the ants to excavate any other region of the stem, they would encounter toxic mucilage that could flood the chamber. Thus, the plant has evolved to provide a home, a specific entranceway and a source of food. A second food reward, so-called pearl glands, which produce a slightly different but equally nutritious meal for the ants, are produced on the leaf-backs and petioles of the youngest leaves. These appear to encourage more frequent and wider-ranging foraging behaviour in the ants. This presumably further reduces predation by foliage eaters, especially on the tenderest, most vulnerable leaves. Embaúba is certainly successful and less bothered by vines and foliage eaters than other trees. The proof, as they say, is in the eating of the pudding.

Survival of the fittest was once a popular catchphrase for

natural selection, but it appears that the struggle for life is considerably more nuanced than once imagined. Mutualism – survival of the cleverest and most cooperative – often wins the day.

INDIAN BEAN TREE

Catalpa bignonioides

Trees in the genus *Catalpa* belong to the Bignoniaceae, a largely tropical family containing mainly woody plants with a cosmopolitan distribution. Catalpas have heart-shaped leaves, widely branched inflorescences and fruits held in long, narrow pods, hence the 'bean trees' moniker. The Indian bean tree (*C. bignonioides*) is one of the most familiar species in the genus, its specific epithet a reference to the floral similarity to those of the climber *Bignonia*.

The Indian bean tree is native to a small part of the south-eastern United States, while a second species, *Catalpa speciosa*, occurs naturally in an area further north in the US, where the two are known as northern and southern catalpa respectively. In the absence of flowers or fruit, the two can be distinguished by the scent of their bruised foliage – *C. bignonioides* emits a foulish odour, while *C. speciosa* does not. Four catalpa species are found in the Caribbean region, while the remaining three or more occur in parts of eastern Asia. These include *C. fargesii* f. *duclouxii*, or Ducloux's catalpa, whose impressive seed pods are up to a metre long.

Both US species have been planted well beyond their native ranges, on both sides of the Atlantic, and old-looking specimens (the species is not particularly long-lived outside of its native range) are often encountered in European parks and gardens. Propped and pruned examples grow outside the Houses of Parliament in central London, while mature specimens can also be found in suburban pockets of several cities, planted in what appears to have been a short-lived trend. The durable timber of *Catalpa* species has been used for railway sleepers in North America, where it has been somewhat shunned as an ornamental in recent years, owing to a somewhat untidy form and seemingly problematic leaf litter (their large leaves, once fallen, can obstruct pavements and block drains, so tidier, usually smaller-leaved alternatives are preferred).

The deciduous leaves of the Indian bean tree are typically the size of dinner plates and usually held oppositely or in whorls of three at the branch tips, with one leaf often smaller than the other two. Juvenile, vigorous shoots produce larger leaves, particularly in response to damage or heavy pruning. It shares this character with other, similarly leaved species in the genus *Paulownia*, known as foxglove trees, though their leaves can be even larger, sometimes up to a metre long!

There is no such thing as a lazy tree, but the Indian bean tree gives the impression of having a somewhat laidback personality; its leaves often emerge late, as spring turns to summer, steering it well clear of the risk of untimely frosts. They are also early to fall in autumn, offering nothing in the way of autumn colour.

They are far from dull, however; a closer look at the leaves reveals a thin layer of hairs spread across the lower surface and particularly along the veins, while in the junctions of primary and secondary veins are extrafloral nectaries – nectar-secreting glands that are not associated with flowers. Possessed by all *Catalpa* species, these appear as smooth, hairless dots that can be green, purplish or nearly black. Catalpa flowers are often visited by bees, who have also been seen to enjoy some extra, leaf-secreted nectar.

Many plants offer nectar away from their floral parts and the topic has long been of great interest to biologists, with the World List of Plants with Extrafloral Nectaries recording them in over 4,000 species in more than 100 families. In different species they occur on different parts, including leaf blades, petioles and stipules, in order to attract arthropods that can protect the developing structures near the nectaries, in return for a carbohydrate-rich food source.

The Indian bean tree attracts highly organised ants to its leaves to provide specific protection against the catalpa sphinx (*Ceratomia catalpa*), which is not a mythical creature but a caterpillar that feeds exclusively on catalpa trees. Infestations can be serious, and specimens may be entirely defoliated as a result. All species of catalpa are considered susceptible, and so all possess extrafloral nectaries, which provide a key source of defence. When their leaves sense damage from the catalpa sphinx moth caterpillars, production of nectar increases dramatically specifically in areas subject to attack, in turn attracting more ants to these leaves. Acting as bodyguards, and keen to protect their own food source, the ants work quickly to chase off the caterpillars.

As well as possessing nectaries, the leaves develop defence

chemicals, including compounds called iridoid glycosides that are stored inside the cells. One of these is catalpol, so named for *Catalpa*, in which it was first discovered, although it is present in several plant species. Bitter-tasting and with growth-inhibiting properties for would-be predators, some iridoid glycosides have anti-feedant properties (azadirachtin, for example, which occurs in neem, see page 47). Effective against insect herbivory, iridoid glycosides do not however deter the caterpillars, who may rather benefit themselves by accumulating catalpol levels within their bodies and subsequently deterring their predators, as has been observed in other caterpillars consuming catalpol-rich leaves. A horticultural selection called 'Catambra' is believed to possess particularly high levels of catalpol and, given its qualities in deterring insects, is marketed as a mosquito-repelling tree in Italy.

While a significant pest to catalpa trees, the catalpa sphinx has been found to make excellent fish bait, and in parts of the southern United States catalpa trees have been grown specifically to attract them (among fisherman they are known as as fishbait trees). This is a brutal life for the trees as, while their leaves are being eaten, they are also being struck with sticks on their trunks and branches by the fisherman as a means to dislodge and harvest the caterpillars. It is a measure of the resilience of the trees that they are able to bounce back and produce leaves season after season, though the perpetual stress and injury does have lasting effects.

Fortunately for the tree, as well as the aid of the ants the catalpa sphinx has a natural predator that helps to keep population levels in check. A parasitic wasp (*Cotesia congregata*) injects the caterpillar with a disabling venom and then lays its eggs along the caterpillar's back. Once they hatch, they feed directly on the caterpillar and eventually kill it, doing their bit to maintain a finely balanced ecological community.

BULLHORN ACACIA

Vachellia cornigera

Though catalpas and cecropias have developed highly specialised, mutualistic relationships with army-forming ants, they are far from unique in these arrangements; at least a quarter of the world's plant families contain species that employ ants either for defence or as aids to pollination. While several members of the pea family, Fabaceae, have leaves rich in alkaloids that defend them from potential predators, given the size of the family – 19,000 or so species – it is not surprising that among its number are plants that are myrmecophilous. The Mesoamerican bullhorn acacia is one, and, like other acacia relatives, it employs ants for protection though, as always, these adept insects don't do it for nothing.

Bullhorn acacia is a small tree, or sometimes only a shrub, with a broad, spreading form. Its standout feature is arguably the pair of fierce, woody spines that subtend each leaf. These are, technically, modified stipules that are fused and lignified.

Slightly flattened towards the tips, and inflated at their conjoined base, they are reddish-brown or sometimes yellowish. Though effective for providing defence against mammalian herbivores, they are equally important for providing domatia (homes) for so-called acacia ants (*Pseudomyrmex* species). These lay their eggs and subsequently raise their young in the hollow cavities inside the spiny domatia. Until recently the 160 or so species of *Vachellia* were part of *Acacia*; thus the ants, which are common to both, retain the common name.

As intricate as any ant–plant interaction, the bullhorn acacia–ant association is initiated when a queen ant, recently mated, spies an unoccupied plant with immature stipules that have not yet fully hardened. With the help of her offspring workers, she burrows into these stipular spines, where she then lays her eggs. These hatch and, as the ant colony expands, additional spiny domatia are inhabited and the ants begin to work as tree protectors. After three or so years, a colony can contain an impressive 16,000 workers, and these patrol the tree's fine branches around the clock, prepared to fend off any potential predators. No trespasser is too large for the diminutive yet determined ants, and they are usually incredibly efficient in driving away those in search of a meal by biting and stinging, with painful or even fatal consequences. Single-minded in the extreme, if they pick up an unfamiliar scent in the tree's vicinity they will appear at the scene, en masse, in seconds, and deal with whatever is getting too close for comfort. They even scour the ground around the tree to see off competitors at that level, be they animal or plant. A bullhorn acacia with a 'weed-free' ring around its base is not an uncommon sight. Once the ant colony gets to around 30,000 strong, some members will spread to neighbouring trees, though the queen usually stays on her original shoot.

Being out on patrol at all hours is of course hungry work. In return for their continuous security, bullhorn acacia rewards its ants with food, which is conveniently located on the leaves that they protect. As is typical for the pea family, the leaves are compound and, in this case, twice-pinnate, with multiple pairs of small pinnules held on the secondary leaf stems. At the tips of these pinnules are small, detachable tips, known as Beltian bodies. Also present in other *Vachellia* and *Acacia* species, they are small structures filled with lipids, sugars and proteins. In bullhorn acacia the bodies are yellowish, orange or sometimes red in colour. They were named after the English naturalist Thomas Belt (1832–1878), who described the mutualistic relationship between bullhorn acacia species and their protective ants.

As the food bodies are particularly important for growing ant larvae, adults remove them and stack them inside the domatia for the larvae to feed on. The adults then feed on another of the leaves' treats – sugary liquid from extrafloral nectaries located at the base of the leaf stem. Although less protein-rich than the Beltian bodies, nectar provides more than adequate sustenance for the ants to go about their work.

Experiments have shown that without their ants, bullhorn acacias fare rather badly. In fact, neither can survive for long without the other. Having lost the ability to produce the alkaloids that are normally present in its relatives, the trees require some other form of protection from herbivores, and equally the ants require a steady source of food and somewhere to lay their eggs and raise their young.

It is therefore a successful, mutually beneficial relationship

– except that there is a predator that is apparently unaware of the script, and this interloper has the ability to evade the ants and utilise the tree for food in a way that other species cannot. *Bagheera kiplingi* is a type of jumping spider, named after the panther in Rudyard Kipling's *The Jungle Book*. Like Bagheera, this spider is noted for its athleticism. It uses its nimbleness to exploit the ant–bullhorn acacia mutualism by robbing the Beltian bodies from the pinnule tips before the ants can get to them. The spiders even snatch the bodies from the ants as they transport them back to feed their young. These artful ant-dodgers hang out on less well-patrolled parts of the tree's crown, darting through the tree in search of their next free meal at the expense of the hard-working ants. From the spider's perspective, eight legs are better than six.

This particular jumping spider, whose range conveniently overlaps that of the bullhorn acacia and its ant-hosting relatives, was one of the first recorded herbivorous arachnids. But it is not exclusively vegetarian and, given the chance, will consume acacia ant larvae as well. Though intricate mutualism works for some, others opt for opportunistic omnivory.

DEFINING LANDSCAPES

Nature can be so soothing to the tormented mind.

ALEXANDER HUMBOLDT

Few places can be as inspiring as those untouched by human inter-ference, but these are, of course, increasingly rare environments. North America's boreal-montane region conceals a multitude of human incursions by virtue of its vastness. Here quaking aspen takes centre stage, and even applauds its own leafy displays. Modified landscapes are the norm nearly everywhere, but if well established are often seen as natural or unchanged. And when the plants within them are remarkable because of appealing architec-ture, or the feel or finish of their leaves, they end up defining landscapes in a way that people will take to heart. Horse chestnut is one such presence. Balkan by birth, it has been transplanted by horticulture across Europe, where it has, until recently, seemingly been at home. The London plane, too, is an interloper, but one that we consciously invited to grace our cities and towns, in part, for the durability of its leaves. But not all landscape-defining plants are welcome. Both Queensland umbrella tree and velvet tree have beautiful leaves, but they are pernicious weeds and insidious reminders that ultimately we are not, nor ever have been, in control of nature.

QUEENSLAND UMBRELLA TREE

Schefflera actinophylla

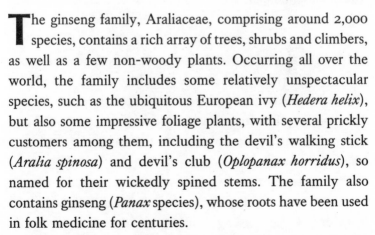

The ginseng family, Araliaceae, comprising around 2,000 species, contains a rich array of trees, shrubs and climbers, as well as a few non-woody plants. Occurring all over the world, the family includes some relatively unspectacular species, such as the ubiquitous European ivy (*Hedera helix*), but also some impressive foliage plants, with several prickly customers among them, including the devil's walking stick (*Aralia spinosa*) and devil's club (*Oplopanax horridus*), so named for their wickedly spined stems. The family also contains ginseng (*Panax* species), whose roots have been used in folk medicine for centuries.

Several of the showy-leaved members of the ginseng family belong to *Schefflera*, the largest genus in the family, which contains somewhere around 1,000 species. Distributed throughout the tropics and subtropics in both hemispheres, they are evergreen shrubs and trees with stout, sparsely branched stems. Scheffleras exhibit palmately compound leaves, often with exceptionally long petioles, and spoke-like secondary petioles that fan out from the tip of the primary leaf stems. The leaflets themselves come in a variety of sizes, the largest, in some tropical species, extending to more than half a metre; petioles can be even twice that length.

The Queensland umbrella tree is among the most familiar of all the scheffleras, as it is both a common landscape subject in the tropics and subtropics, including around popular resort hotels, and also a stalwart, shade-tolerant indoor plant, much used in offices and shopping malls across the world. For a *Schefflera*, Queensland umbrella tree has modest-sized leaves, held on stout petioles with glossy, oblong leaflets. The specific epithet, *actinophylla*, means 'with radiating leaves', which is true of all scheffleras, while 'umbrella tree' could also equally apply to any member of the genus. In its wild range, which includes tropical forested habitats from southern New Guinea to northern Australia, the Queensland umbrella tree starts out a shrub and eventually becomes a multi-trunked tree. Plants may also grow as epiphytes, perched on other trees or shrubs. As epiphytes, their roots are capable of wrapping around and smothering smaller host plants, but the species is not in any way truly parasitic.

The umbrella tree has few significant pests in nature, primarily because of its interesting internal chemistry. All members of the ginseng family have distinctive aromatic compounds in their tissues, and they mostly smell strongly of ivy (*Hedera*), especially when handled. The aromatic compounds that produce these scents are mostly toxic, but usually not gravely so. They are usually bitter enough to dissuade potential wild herbivores from continuing to sample much of the foliage. Significantly, though, the presence of irritating calcium oxalate crystals in *Schefflera* tissues renders them quite dangerous for mammals, including pets encountering indoor plants. The crystals, or raphides, get stuck in the tissues of the mouth and can cause significant pain and swelling. As a result, we would consider the plant essentially inedible. But don't tell Bennett's tree kangaroo (*Dendrolagus bennettianus*) – this elusive and near-threatened marsupial native to Queensland's lowland tropical rainforests is known to feed on the foliage with no ill effects.

Queensland umbrella tree is a common 'escape' (from cultivation) in tropical regions and has naturalised in places like the Pacific and Caribbean islands and the Canaries. Its ability to establish quickly with aggressive roots and prolific above-ground growth, its broad environmental tolerances and especially its bird-dispersed seeds, all contribute to the species' invasive behaviour. Of course, many of the same characteristics make it a resilient and popular indoor plant, although as noted, the toxic leaves make them unsuited to pets and, heaven forbid, babies who might chew on them. Like the millions of butterfly palms, weeping figs and corn plants sold by home-decor retailers, Queensland umbrella tree is an easy, fast-growing plant, common to large ornamental greenhouse crop producers around the world.

The arrangement of the leaflets and position of the leaves allows the Queensland umbrella tree, as well as other scheffleras, to maximise their photosynthetic surface area, while reducing self-shading. Much of the adaptability of the species to different environments is due to this foliar versatility. At the start of new growth in spring the petioles ascend stiffly, as the unexpanded leaflets hang downward, away from direct sunshine. Both petiole angle and leaflet attitude are variable, and where plants are exposed to the full force of the tropical sun, petioles tend to be shorter and nearly upright with the leaflets remaining vertical to avoid overheating or burning. In shade, both the petiole and leaflet angle generally adjust themselves closer to the horizontal. Indoor scheffleras frequently exhibit this pattern of growth. Stalk length is also somewhat variable, especially with heavily shaded plants, the petioles and secondary petioles often extending significantly. Like most other ginseng relatives, schefflera leaves have broad, clasping petiole bases and, when a leaf naturally falls away, a large, diamond-shaped leaf scar remains. The unusual size of the leaf attachment is the result of the fusion of the petiole base with stipular tissues, which form a membranous ear-like edge on either side of the petiole.

While it is the leaves of scheffleras that generally appeal, their flowers are worthy of attention too. Most species bear small flowers in crown-like inflorescences at the apex of the current season's shoots, and *S. actinophylla* does not disappoint in this regard; though indoor plants would never be expected to produce flowers. The inflorescences of the Queensland umbrella tree are celebrated for their striking, multiple upright, curving, burgundy-red stalks, buds and flowers. This arrangement gives the species its other common name: octopus plant. The flowers are pollinated by all manner of bees and flies, and the purple-red berries that follow are exceptionally attractive to fruit-eating bats and birds.

The name *Schefflera* commemorates the Polish-Prussian eighteenth-century physician and naturalist Johann Peter

Ernst von Scheffler (1739–1809). Although Scheffler seems never to have ventured beyond Europe, nor actually encountered a *Schefflera* in the flesh, he was evidently a much-esteemed physician and botanist and considered worthy of the honorific name.

HORSE CHESTNUT

Aesculus hippocastanum

I n Europe, horse chestnut is widespread and so common that it is often assumed to be indigenous over much of the continent. However, it is in fact originally native only to limited areas in sheltered valleys of the Balkans in southern Europe. The tree's familiarity is the result of its extensive cultivation as an ornamental since the seventeenth century. In flower, it is one of the most spectacular of any large temperate tree. The inflorescences appear after the leaves have fully expanded in spring, sitting candelabrum-like throughout the crown and pollinated by bees. Hanging clusters of soft-prickly fruits follow in summer. These eventually fall and split to expose glossy brown, rounded seeds, the 'conkers' of playground fame, much beloved by children. In winter trees are easily distinguished by their large, arching boughs, tipped with stout twigs and large, very sticky buds.

So popular is horse chestnut in the United Kingdom that

in 2017 it was voted the region's favourite tree. It is also widely grown across parts of western Asia, India and North America, with cultivated and naturalised populations considerably over-shadowing those in the Balkans; these are thought to amount to no more than 10,000 trees, while the UK population alone comprises nearly half a million specimens.

Along with the maples (*Acer*), the horse chestnuts belong to the Hippocastanoideae subfamily within the soapberry family, Sapindaceae. Their most obvious similarity to the maples is their oppositely arranged twigs and buds, though most other members of the soapberry family have alternately arranged buds and, again, unlike maples and horse chestnuts, the family is predominantly tropical.

There are a little more than a dozen horse chestnut species globally, with *Aesculus hippocastanum* the only species native to Europe. The others occur in parts of North America and southern and eastern Asia. All have palmately compound leaves, with those of the European horse chestnut typically comprising seven large, oblong leaflets that broaden towards their tips before narrowing abruptly to a short point. These are prominently veined and have toothed edges.

Horse chestnuts are vigorous trees and, under optimal conditions, can put on nearly a metre in growth each year. It is one of the first common temperate trees to leaf out in spring and promptly puts on a surprising burst of new growth. The rich green of the new leaves and stems is covered with fluffy, orange-coloured hairs, though these are shed as the leaves gradually unfold and expand. For more than 200 years horse chestnuts have played a prominent role in managed environments and have been much adored arboreal elements of the landscape. Sadly, while embodying such promise in spring, the prevailing image of the horse chestnut in much of Europe is now one of a tired, somewhat battered-looking tree that is soon past its best. By July or August autumn appears to have already arrived for these magnificent trees, their leaves increasingly brown and crinkled and already falling to the ground. They are being attacked by the larvae of a tiny, leaf-mining moth that, to the detriment of its helpless host, makes a home within its leaves.

The moth (*Cameraria ohridella*) was discovered in Macedonia in the 1970s and has come to be known as the horse chestnut leaf miner. Since that time, it has spread at an impressive rate – up to 100 kilometres a year – across much of Europe. In spring, female moths lay their eggs on the upper surface of the leaves, the tiny caterpillar hatchlings soon excavating mines, feeding on the sap from leaf veins. This causes disfiguring brown blotches to form across the foliage from summer onwards, eventually causing leaves to drop prematurely.

Under warm, dry conditions, the moth can produce up to five generations a year, with the last of them (and likely a few hangers-on from earlier in the year) overwintering as pupae in the fallen leaves, poised to produce a new generation for the next year. Once new leaves are fully developed the following spring, there is plenty for them to feed on, so the cycle goes around again. Damage is usually first observed on the lower branches, while successive generations feed on leaves further and further up the crown. As a warming climate enables the moth to produce additional generations, completely ravaged trees in late summer are becoming more and more familiar. A suggested treatment is to remove fallen leaves from beneath trees in winter, which clears the moth pupae along with them. While this may be achievable in urban environments, it is impractical and near impossible in woodlands and wild environments, including within the native range of horse chestnut, where the moth also occurs.

The impact of the moth is lessened only by its seasonality, with most infestations becoming established after trees have already completed much of their yearly photosynthetic exertion. Still, it is estimated that the moth reduces annual carbon assimilation by up to 40 per cent, which is enough to eventually take a toll on the vitality of the tree. A stressed tree is a weakened tree and its ability to fight off further disease is reduced. Fruit production can be seriously impacted, with seeds of infested trees sometimes only half the size of a normal seed. Small seeds are of course a problem for children playing conkers, but are a far bigger issue for the species in the wild; seed germination is frequently limited and those that 'succeed' are often runts, unlikely to make it to maturity themselves. Infested trees may also produce fewer female flowers, which presents a further hurdle to reproduction.

As if one leaf problem wasn't bad enough, horse chestnuts are also commonly infected by a leaf blotch fungus (*Guignardia aesculi*) that disfigures the leaves. Strangely, the resultant damage is similar to that caused by the leaf miner, with infected leaves growing increasingly blotched and deformed as the season progresses. Favouring wetter conditions than the leaf miner, the fungus too can be managed in garden environments by removing fallen leaves, which are a source of infecting spores, though again this is no guarantee of preventing reinfection.

And it is not only the leaves of horse chestnuts that are subjected to disease. Another worrying malady, known as bleeding canker, can also be a problem. Infection causes an ugly discharge of sticky sap from wounds on the trunks of established older trees and eventually leads to dieback of the crown. At least two organisms are responsible for the canker disease – the bacterium *Pseudomonas syringae* pv. *aesculi* and, in Europe, the water mould *Phytophthora plurivora*.

While there is a mounting burden of pests and diseases afflicting horse chestnut today, the risks to the native Balkan populations are greater still. Human impacts in the form of mountain tourism, wildfires and illegal logging are presenting significant threats to the species in the wild. The future of this old favourite, currently listed as Vulnerable on the IUCN Red List, is decidedly uncertain.

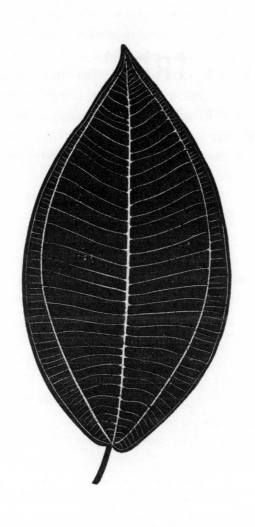

VELVET TREE

Miconia calvescens

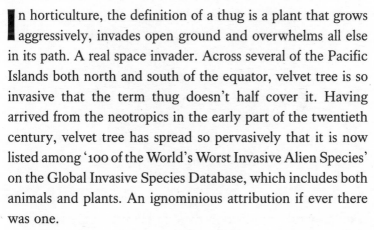

In horticulture, the definition of a thug is a plant that grows aggressively, invades open ground and overwhelms all else in its path. A real space invader. Across several of the Pacific Islands both north and south of the equator, velvet tree is so invasive that the term thug doesn't half cover it. Having arrived from the neotropics in the early part of the twentieth century, velvet tree has spread so pervasively that it is now listed among '100 of the World's Worst Invasive Alien Species' on the Global Invasive Species Database, which includes both animals and plants. An ignominious attribution if ever there was one.

Miconia calvescens is a small tree native to parts of Central and South America, from Mexico south to Argentina, where it forms part of the forest understorey. One look at its hugely ornamental leaf and it's obvious that it belongs to the melastome family, Melastomataceae. Two prominent veins diverge from the base of the wide midrib and arch elegantly, roughly paralleling the margins, ultimately meeting at the leaf tip. There is ladder-like cross-veining between the main veins, much like in the leaves of trotroka (*Dichaetanthera cordifolia*); this is a characteristic feature of the melastomes. Unlike trotroka, its leaves are immense – up to a metre long – and the veins are white and prominent against the lustrous green background. The leaf undersides are either green or purple, and the purple form looks particularly rich – like velvet – which gives the tree its common name. The specific epithet, *calvescens*, roughly translates as 'becoming bold'. As the leaves expand and shed their stellate hairs, the surface transforms from subtle to spectacular. Botanical specimens suggest that the green form predominates across large parts of tropical South America, whereas purple-leaved plants were originally restricted to parts of Central America.

It was for its distinctive foliar characteristics that velvet tree was originally cultivated, first under glass in Europe in the middle of the eighteenth century, then later as an exotic tropical ornamental at a botanic garden in Tahiti (French Polynesia) in 1937. Velvet tree was first observed as invasive in natural areas there in the 1970s. The species now grows across nearly two-thirds of the island, forming dense, uninterrupted stands over around a quarter of the territory in areas of abundant rainfall, where it threatens to displace nearly 100 native plant species. Velvet tree arrived in Hawaii in the 1960s – it was also intentionally introduced for its ornamental qualities – and was widely sold before its noxious qualities were recognised, too late, in the early 1990s. Though not as speciose as Madagascar, levels of plant endemism on Hawaii are similar to those of the African island, and its native species are similarly vulnerable. A worrying 10 per cent of the Hawaiian flora has gone extinct since the mid-1800s, with over half of the remaining species considered at risk of extinction. Invasive species are considered the primary threat. As in Tahiti, native plants in areas of high rainfall are most vulnerable to being outcompeted by the velvet tree.

The species is also invasive in the Society and Marquesas islands (French Polynesia), parts of New Caledonia and in tropical Queensland, Australia. It is naturalised in parts of the Caribbean, and while its status in parts of Southeast Asia is not well documented, its potential to wreak havoc there is a cause for concern. In tropical forests of Asia, fellow melastome and neotropical native soapbush or Koster's curse (*Clidemia hirta*) has successfully invaded closed-canopy forests across a number of countries. That species is also a significant problem in Hawaii and also makes the '100 of the World's Worst Invasive Alien Species' list.

Velvet tree has several characteristics that have led to its invasiveness. It is well-adapted to low light levels, with seeds that can germinate and grow in near darkness as they wait for a gap in the canopy. When the opportunity arrives, they are able to grow rapidly into available space, putting on more than a metre in growth every year. As they grow taller, their large, dark leaves shade out all that lies beneath them, eliminating the seedlings of other species. The soil beneath the leaves then becomes bare and exposed, and thus vulnerable to erosion in periods of heavy rainfall. Further, velvet tree only produces very shallow roots, which exacerbate the risk of erosion and increase the likelihood of landslides on unstable ground.

Velvet tree plants reach sexual maturity after just four or

five years, when they begin to flower and fruit. And prolifically so. A single plant bears more than 200 inflorescences, which can each produce more than 200 fruits. Within each fruit are around 200 seeds. Add to this that plants can flower up to three times annually and you see that they have the potential to produce astronomical numbers of seedlings each year, which they do. Unsurprisingly, velvet tree can very quickly transform entire ecosystems. Small wonder that alternative names for it include 'purple plague'. The French name for the plant is 'cancer vert' (green cancer).

The fruits of the velvet tree are often eaten and its seeds dispersed by birds, which serves to increase its spread. The seeds are also easily transported by travelling on the bottom of shoes or tyres, as well as being spread by wind and water. The fruits themselves don't travel far without these aids, as they tend to fall close to parent trees. In dense stands, this leads to the accumulation of huge quantities of seeds, which remain viable in the ground for nearly a decade, ready to re-invade should the removal of mature trees be carried out in attempts to eliminate velvet tree populations.

Controlling the spread of the velvet tree is thus a huge (and expensive) challenge, with the possibility of intended remedial actions making a bad situation worse by further unbalancing ecosystems at inherent risk. On Hawaii and the Society Islands, the velvet tree is targeted by the defoliating Chinese rose beetle (*Adoretus sinicus*), itself another invasive species now widespread in parts of Southeast Asia and the Pacific Islands. The introduction of this species was unintentional; it was thought to have arrived on plant material imported for the ornamental or timber trades. While the beetle is capable of stripping individual velvet trees of up to half of their leaves, it isn't considered a significant danger to the species. Unfortunately, it is yet another threat to the native flora. Within the velvet tree's native range, moths that feed on its fruit limit its reproduction, though to trial the moth's utility as a biological control in a new environment carries further environmental risk and similar experiments have previously proved unsuccessful. To manage such fragile, damaged ecosystems back to their natural state, as far as is possible, is a colossal task, albeit one that is absolutely necessary.

ORIENTAL PLANE

Platanus orientalis

With one exception – plane trees – in the genus *Platanus*, have leaves that are broad, palmately lobed and superficially like those of common maple (*Acer*) species. Indeed, botanist and godfather of modern botanical nomenclature, Carl Linnaeus (1707–1778), named the genus for the way its leaves are held in a flat plane. He also named two maples for their likeness to the planes. The specific epithet of the Norway maple (*Acer platanoides*) translates as 'plane-like' and that of the European sycamore (*Acer pseudoplatanus*) means 'false plane'. They are certainly close in leaf morphology, with the key to not confusing these common trees in the absence of flowers being in how the leaves are arranged.

Leaves, or more accurately their buds, are arranged either oppositely, alternately or in whorls. Maples have oppositely arranged leaves, while those of plane trees are positioned alternately along the stem. Another tree genus, *Liquidambar*, the sweet gums, also has species with maple-like leaves, which too are alternately arranged. However, most plane tree leaves have a further character that quickly distinguishes them from both these genera: the base of the leaf stem, the petiole, is distinctly swollen and encloses the next year's developing bud within it. Plane trees also have prominent stipules that protect the developing leaves, though these are soon shed once the leaves are fully enlarged.

There are somewhere between six and ten plane species (the vagueness is the result of differing taxonomic opinion among genus specialists). The majority are distributed across temperate parts of the United States and Mexico. There are two exceptions in the genus. *Platanus kerrii*, which has unlobed leaves and buds not enclosed by petioles, is from tropical regions of Laos and Vietnam. The only temperate plane naturally occurring within the Eastern Hemisphere is oriental plane. However, to what precise region it is truly native has become difficult to trace with certainty, owing to it having been moved around so much. The species' natural distribution is generally accepted to include parts of south-east Europe, eastwards to the Caucasus, though the eastern and western extent of that range is somewhat unclear.

The principal reason for its intentional spreading is in its value as a shade tree. One of the largest, longest-lived trees of the eastern Mediterranean region, and possessing huge, sweeping boughs, oriental plane has been revered since classical antiquity. Indeed, Hippocrates is believed to have taught medicine beneath a plane on the Greek island of Kos in the sixth century BCE. That tree, or at least a sprout from it, is still alive and is a site of pilgrimage for big tree lovers and medical people alike. Cuttings from it are propagated and grown at sites as far away as Canada and New Zealand.

Napoleon is credited with the planting of plane trees along French roads so that his army could march in the shade, though many plantings date from the reign of Henri IV in the sixteenth century.

Pliny the Elder mentions that as well as shade, the leaves of the oriental plane, when at their freshest and boiled with white wine, can be used to treat eye irritations. A tea concocted from the leaves is also reputed to be effective in treating joint problems, and other plant parts have also been used to remedy various ailments, though its use as a shade tree appears to have prevailed above these purposes. The leaves of the species are always distinctly five-lobed and often deeply so, though this varies to some extent, with lobe depth and degree of toothing frequently showing regional differences.

In western Europe, oriental plane is most encountered as one of the parents of the hybrid London plane (*Platanus* x *hispanica*). The other parent is the western plane of eastern North America – also known as buttonwood or American sycamore (*P. occidentalis*). Though *occidentalis* translates as 'western', this relates to its distribution compared with the eastern oriental plane, rather than its range within North America. *Platanus occidentalis* is a component of riparian forests and, as it grows to heights of more than 50 metres, is one of the tallest broadleaved trees in North America. The western plane has shallowly lobed leaves, while those of its hybrid offspring are intermediate between its parents. With a vigour frequently seen in hybrids of all kinds, London plane makes one of the largest broadleaved trees in Europe and the oldest examples have yet to stop growing. Specimens of *P.* x *hispanica* are valued not only for the shade they cast, but for a wide range of ecosystem services. One of London's oldest examples, growing in Berkeley Square, was valued at £750,000 in 2009.

Growing in and around London since the late 1700s, London plane has proven to be incredibly tolerant of urban environments. Some specimens have endured over two centuries' worth of particulate pollution. This is no insignificant burden considering the choking amounts of soot from wood and especially coal burning throughout much of London in the last three centuries. Their admirable ability to withstand airborne toxins is largely thanks to their exfoliating bark, which, as it is periodically shed, ensures that its lenticels remain clear enough to perform their essential function of gas exchange. Still, the deleterious effects of the urban environment do have an impact. Airborne pollutants decrease chlorophyll production and reduce the size of leaves. But although their function is affected, the durable leaves of plane trees are still able to perform well enough.

No tree is perfect, and plane trees can be troublesome for some. When the leaves emerge in spring they are covered in tiny hairs. When the tree sheds them later, they can cause breathing difficulties if inhaled, and the same issue is caused by the ageing, disassembling fruit clusters. Shedding hairs is less problematic in damper climates, and even though the potential for respiratory trouble has been known for centuries, plane trees have seemingly always been widely planted. Time will tell whether the changing climate will exacerbate the problem and thus give urban planners a new arboreal challenge.

Aside from the leaves, the abundant pollen of the London plane can also be an irritant, even to those seemingly immune to hay fever. On breezy May days, city parks can be thick with plane pollen and unexpected bouts of sneezing can often be attributed to plane trees nearby. Though intolerable to some in spring, as the days heat up and people flock to the parks, visitors seek out the shade of the plane trees.

QUAKING ASPEN

Populus tremuloides

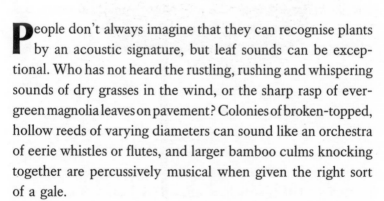

People don't always imagine that they can recognise plants by an acoustic signature, but leaf sounds can be exceptional. Who has not heard the rustling, rushing and whispering sounds of dry grasses in the wind, or the sharp rasp of evergreen magnolia leaves on pavement? Colonies of broken-topped, hollow reeds of varying diameters can sound like an orchestra of eerie whistles or flutes, and larger bamboo culms knocking together are percussively musical when given the right sort of a gale.

What about the quaking aspen? The sound of this tree's leaves in the wind has been described as everything from 'running water' to 'a gentle crackling', to 'the rising and falling of a passing rain shower'. It is a relaxing, if not actually meditative sound to those who hear it, and is probably a perfect candidate for 'white noise' recordings. White noise is basically a sonically dense, fuzzy sound, where separate high and low frequencies are not discernible. Artificially produced white noise is sometimes used in offices to drown out traffic and other distracting random noises, and can help people relax or focus. Hikers often describe the experience of being around quaking aspen in full leaf as both calming and uplifting. Yet as enjoyable as the sound might be, there doesn't appear to be any actual purpose to it.

Quaking aspen, also known as trembling aspen, is a small, usually single-stemmed tree. Despite the low quality of its wood, it is one of the most important timber trees in North America. The wood is used for a variety of applications, the most important of which, monetarily, is in particleboard, especially oriented strandboard. Native to cool northern and montane habitats from the Arctic to Mexico, the species has one of the largest ranges of any North American deciduous tree and is famous for its exceptional colonising tendencies. Quaking aspen has a soboliferous habit, which is to say that new plants sprout readily from spreading roots. Individual sprouts are known as ramets, and the interconnected root system an ortet. As all the ramets from one ortet are genetically identical, they represent clonal colonies, and some individual colonies are composed of hundreds or even tens of thousands of separate ramets. One quaking aspen colony located in Utah, which is known as Pando (Latin for 'I spread'), occupies over 40 hectares. There are more than 40,000 ramets in Pando, and the total weight has been estimated at 6,000 tonnes, making it the most massive organism on earth. Although the lifespan of an individual ramet is usually less than 130 years, the ortet is probably many thousands of years old. The soboliferous lifestyle is an effective adaptation for surviving periodic forest fires, and other above-ground catastrophes. Colonies in fire-prone areas are often represented by even-aged ramets, indicating that trees are frequently destroyed en masse before individuals would normally die and be replaced by localised regenerants.

Aspens, along with the cottonwoods and poplars, are all subgroups in the genus *Populus*, and members of the willow family, Salicaceae. Like the willows, poplars are typically fast-growing, soft-wooded deciduous trees that favour wet, open sites, and quaking aspens are specifically adapted to the moisture that derives from winter snow cover. Poplars are native throughout the temperate Northern Hemisphere. The species are all wind-pollinated, the flowers of both sexes borne in catkins on separate trees. The famous Pando colony, for example, is a male clone.

Perhaps more than any other feature, quaking aspens are known for their smooth, chalky grey-white bark. While never truly white, the bark on older trees is interrupted by dark, horizontal lenticels and widely spaced, black, irregularly diamond-shaped branch scars that make the lightness of the bark stand out in sharp contrast. Very old trees have darkening bark that is roughly furrowed, but only near the ground. The crown habit of most quaking aspen is usually oval to rounded, but often sparse and open, with only a few secondary branches arising from the main stem. This structure allows snow to readily accumulate at the base of the tree.

The spirally arranged leaves of quaking aspen are broad, and rounded to heart-shaped, but small compared with other poplars. They are dark green above and glaucous-blue below, and usually have fine to rounded marginal teeth. Aspens exhibit seasonally heterophyllous growth. Seasonal heterophylly (*hetero* = different + *phylly* = leaves) is characterised by different 'early' and 'late' leaves. Early (i.e. first-opened) leaves are derived from pre-formed tissues that overwinter in buds as tightly rolled, unexpanded leaves, while late leaves represent tissues initiated and expanded after the expansion of the early leaves. Typically, a small number of early leaves are crowded at the base of the shoot, while late leaves may be conspicuously larger, more widely spaced along the expanding stem, and often larger and more triangular than the early ones.

The most remarkable feature of the quaking aspen leaf is the petiole, which is flattened at right angles to the plane of the leaf blade and gives it its distinctive fluttering motion. Even in the gentlest breeze, the leaves both oscillate and roll; that is, they move from side to side while simultaneously twisting vertically. The intensity of the sound derives from the degree of fluttering, rather than any rubbing of the leaves or stalks. The leaves are as compelling to watch as they are to hear, and their unusual structure has considerable biological advantages for the tree. Research has shown that the near-constant movement of leaves at the top of the canopy confers an advantage in intercepting the maximum amount of light on individual leaves, compared with leaves that are in fixed positions and thus angled away from the light for long periods. Leaf movement also increases light through the canopy, benefiting leaves that would otherwise be shaded.

Not so well adapted to soggy environments as poplar or willow species, aspens are generally better at tolerating hot, dry conditions. One of the reasons for this drought adaptability is again attributable to the flattened petiole. The near-constant motion of leaves lessens continuous sun exposure and leaf heating, and this is correlated with a reduction in evapotranspiration. Pretty cool.

While there do not appear to be regionally recognisable variations in tree form or summer leaf colour, there are often striking differences between individual clones that only become evident in autumn. This is sometimes spectacularly apparent on mountainsides where there are multiple clonal colonies. Colours can range from soft yellow to brilliant chromium yellow, and occasionally vermillion-orange and pale red.

Quaking aspen are host to a wide range of herbivores. Ungulates (deer, elk, moose, etc.) feed on young shoots year-round. In winter, porcupines, rabbits and other small mammals, elevated by or hidden in the deep snow, feed on the smooth young bark and winter buds. The leaves are sometimes infested by the aspen serpentine leafminer (*Phyllocnistis populiella*), which feeds inside the leaf and causes irregular and often attractive silvery trails across the leaf surface. In some years, the miners can build up to disturbing proportions and cause premature defoliation, though trees invariably recover. Poplar galls, which affect all *Populus* species, are often caused by specialised aphids (*Pemphigus* spp.) that pierce tissues – mostly leaf blades and leaf veins – to lay their eggs. The plant's response is to form a wall of tissue – a gall – around the developing larva. Aphids are not the only insects associated with poplar galls. The petiole poplar gall moth (*Ectoedemia populella*) causes large galls to form on petioles, and these undoubtedly affect the biomechanics of affected quaking aspen leaves. Still, galls, like other damaging agents, have little adverse effect on tree health, especially as even major destruction will be countered with new shoots from the unseen ortet below. Quaking aspens will continue to cause enjoyable fluttering wherever they grow.

ACKNOWLEDGEMENTS

We are grateful to those who helped this book come together. Thanks to Kate Hewson and Kate Craigie at Two Roads for managing to keep us on track, and to Kate Hewson for the original inspiration. To Vanessa Handley for thoughts and suggestions on tree species and for sharing reference images for illustration. Karen Justice for myriad editorial improvements and Susanna Bayliss for informative thoughts on some very early drafts. Thanks to our wives, Sarika (Dan) and Karen (Douglas), for their patience and support throughout the writing process, and of course to trees themselves, for providing a constant source of fascination and inspiration.

GLOSSARY

Alternate: leaves, buds or branches inserted at different levels on an axis; compare with opposite (inserted immediately adjacent to and more or less on opposite sides of the stem; paired).

Arborescent: tree-like.

Armature: modified, often hardened, sharpened plant parts that provide protection.

Bract: a modified protective leaf associated with an inflorescence, with buds or with newly emerging shoots and stems.

Compound leaf: a leaf composed of separate leaflets on a single axis or multiple axes.

Decussate: paired leaves, buds or branches arising at 90 degrees to the pair below.

Epiphyte: a plant that grows upon another plant, but that does not derive any sustenance directly from the host.

Glaucous: of a dull greyish-green or blue colour; coated with bluish powdery wax.

Heterophylly (adj. heterophyllous): variation in leaf shape.

Inflorescence: a flower stalk, including the main stem and all subordinate stems and the flowers.

Lignin: complex organic polymers deposited in the cell walls of plants, making them rigid and woody.

Morphology: description of shape and outward structure.

Ovate: egg-shaped in outline.

Ovoid: three-dimensionally egg-shaped.

Palmate: describing three or more lobes, veins or other structures that radiate away from a central point.

Petiole: the leaf stalk.

Pathogenic: disease-causing.

Phyllotaxy: the arrangement of leaves around the stem.

Pinnately compound: a leaf with a central axis that has separate lateral leaflets arranged on either side of the axis.

Rachis: the central axis of a pinnately compound leaf or fern frond above the petiole.

Senescence: deteriorating with age.

Sepal: a single element in the outermost floral whorl; often green and forming the protective cover of the flower bud in many kinds of plants.

Stipule: a leafy outgrowth, often paired and usually arising at the base of the leaf stalk; sometimes acting as a protective cover for an overwintering bud.

Ungulate: a hoofed mammal.

FURTHER READING

A Natural History of Trees of Eastern and Central North America. Donald Culross Peattie (author) and Paul H. Landacre (illustrations). Boston: Houghton Mifflin, 1966

Conifers of the World: The Complete Reference. James E. Eckenwalder. Portland: Timber Press, 2009

Global Invasive Species Database www.iucngisd.org/gisd

Palms Throughout the World. David L. Jones. Washington, DC: Smithsonian Institution Scholarly Press, 1995

Plants of the World: An Illustrated Encyclopedia of Vascular Plants. Maarten J. M. Christenhusz, Mark Wayne Chase and Michael Francis Fay. Richmond: Kew Publishing, 2017

The IUCN Red List of Threatened Species www.iucnredlist. org

The Tree: A Natural History of What Trees Are, How They Live, and Why They Matter. Colin Tudge. New York: Three Rivers Press, 2005

Trees and Shrubs Online http://treesandshrubsonline.org

Further Reading

Trees, Their Natural History 2nd Edition. Peter Thomas. Cambridge: Cambridge University Press, 2014

Tropical and Subtropical Trees: An Encyclopaedia. Margaret Barwick. Portland: Timber Press, 2004

World list of plants with extrafloral nectaries www.extrafloral nectaries.org. 2015